The Directory of Websites for International Jobs

By Drs. Ron and Caryl Krannich

BUSINESS AND CAREER BOOKS AND SOFTWARE

101 Dynamite Answers to Interview Questions
101 Secrets of Highly Effective Speakers
201 Dynamite Job Search Letters
Best Jobs For the 21st Century
America's Top Internet Job Sites
Change Your Job, Change Your Life
The Complete Guide to International Jobs and Careers
The Complete Guide to Public Employment
The Directory of Federal Jobs and Employers
Discover the Best Jobs For You!
Dynamite Cover Letters
Dynamite Networking For Dynamite Jobs
Dynamite Resumes
Dynamite Salary Negotiations
Dynamite Tele-Search
The Educator's Guide to Alternative Jobs and Careers
Find a Federal Job Fast!
From Air Force Blue to Corporate Gray
From Army Green to Corporate Gray
From Navy Blue to Corporate Gray
Get a Raise in 7 Days
High Impact Resumes and Letters
Interview For Success
Job-Power Source CD-ROM
Jobs and Careers With Nonprofit Organizations
Military Resumes and Cover Letters
Moving Out of Education
Moving Out of Government
Re-Careering in Turbulent Times
Resumes & Job Search Letters For Transitioning Military Personnel
Savvy Interviewing
Savvy Networker
Savvy Resume Writer
Ultimate Job Source CD-ROM

TRAVEL AND INTERNATIONAL BOOKS

Best Resumes and CVs For International Jobs
The Directory of Websites For International Jobs
International Jobs Directory
Jobs For People Who Love to Travel
Mayors and Managers in Thailand
Politics of Family Planning Policy in Thailand
Shopping and Traveling in Exotic Asia
Shopping in Exotic Places
Shopping the Exotic South Pacific
Travel Planning On the Internet
Treasures and Pleasures of Australia
Treasures and Pleasures of China
Treasures and Pleasures of Egypt
Treasures and Pleasures of Hong Kong
Treasures and Pleasures of India
Treasures and Pleasures of Indonesia
Treasures and Pleasures of Italy
Treasures and Pleasures of Mexico
Treasures and Pleasures of Morocco
Treasures and Pleasures of Paris and the French Riviera
Treasures and Pleasures of the Philippines
Treasures and Pleasures of Rio and São Paulo
Treasures and Pleasures of Singapore and Bali
Treasures and Pleasures of Singapore and Malaysia
Treasures and Pleasures of Southern Africa
Treasures and Pleasures of Thailand
Treasures and Pleasures of Vietnam

The Directory of Websites for International Jobs

The Click and Easy™ Guide

Ronald L. Krannich, Ph.D.
Caryl Rae Krannich, Ph.D.

IMPACT PUBLICATIONS
Manassas Park, Virginia

Library of Congress Cataloguing-in-Publication Data

Krannich, Ronald L.
    The directory of websites for international jobs : the click and easy guide / Ron and Caryl Krannich.
        p. cm. – (Click & easy series)
    Includes bibliographical references and index.
    ISBN 1-57023-179-6 (alk. paper)
        1. Americans–Employment–Foreign countries–Computer network resources. 2. Employment in foreign countries–Computer network resources. 3. Job hunting–Computer network resources. 4. Internet. I. Krannich, Caryl Rae. II. Title. III. Series.

HF5549.5.E45 K734 2002
025.06'65014–dc21

                                      2001059423

Contents

IMPACT PUBLICATIONS
The Career & Travel Resource Center
1-800-361-1055 or 703-361-7300

| Home | Career Store | Travel Store | eBooks | Multimedia | Catalogs | Search |

Search Career: HR/Career Mgmt ▼ GO!   Search Travel: Accommodations ▼ GO!

SEARCH&Shop

[GO!]

Login Register

Your Shopping Cart
<Basket Empty>

Login Register

Career & Business Store

CHANGE YOUR JOB Change

Your gateway to today's most useful books, videos, software, and other products relevant to job seekers, employers, and students.

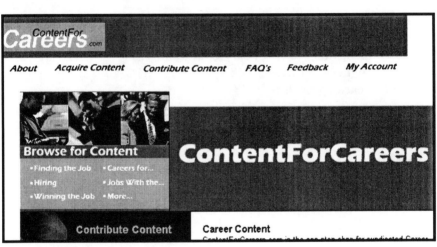

ContentFor Careers.com

About   Acquire Content   Contribute Content   FAQ's   Feedback   My Account

Browse for Content
- Finding the Job
- Careers for...
- Hiring
- Jobs With the...
- Winning the Job
- More...

ContentForCareers

Contribute Content   Career Content

iShopAroundtheWorld.com
The Ultimate in Shopping & Travel

Travel the World. Shop for Treasures.

| Home | Global Shopping Directory | Great Destinations | Books n' More | Travel Tips |

Great Destinations
- Asia
- Europe
- The Americas
- Africa
- Pacific

Global Shopping Directory
- Antiques
- Art
- Carpets
- Clothes/Textiles
- Crafts
- Furniture
- Hotels

── Features ──

Travel-Shopping Destinations

The Treasures and Pleasures of

SINGAPORE

Dynamic, Enterprising Singapore: A

Unique Products & Shops

Ikat Designs from Indonesia

Textiles from Bali

1

Online International Job Finding

TODAY'S GLOBAL ECONOMY OFFERS MANY EXCITING opportunities for enterprising individuals interested in pursuing international jobs and careers as well as for those wishing to experience a fascinating global lifestyle. Whether you want to work in Rio de Janeiro, London, Paris, Rome, Moscow, Cairo, Bangkok, Singapore, Hong Kong, Tokyo, Sydney, San Francisco, New York City, or Washington, DC, with the right set of marketable skills and information on where and how to find the jobs, you should be able to join a growing number of successful job seekers who land their international dream job.

Discover Your Best Friend

Assuming you have marketable international skills and a good sense of how to find a job, the following chapters focus on the where and how of finding an international job by using a variety of useful online resources. Today, the Internet is the international job seeker's best friend. Using the Internet, you can search for job opportunities throughout the world 24 hours a day and in the comfort of your home or office. You can research employers, network for information and advice, explore new opportunities, email your resume and letters, search for job vacancies, contact headhunters, and post your resume to numerous employment databases. Internet-savvy international job seekers constantly use the Internet to move their job search in the right direction – toward job interviews and offers.

A World Wide Web of Opportunities

The purpose of this book is to quickly link you to some of the best websites for conducting an effective international job search. In the following pages you'll find over 1,400 websites that relate to different aspects of the job search and to various international employment arenas. If you explore many of these websites, you'll quickly discover a whole new world of global employment opportunities in business, government, and the nonprofit sector. Indeed, you may soon become addicted to conducting much of your international job search via the Internet. While you should engage in many traditional job search activities, such as skills assessment, interpersonal networking, and mailing resumes, by all means incorporate the Internet into your job search. The many online resources identified in this book can greatly enhance your more traditional job search activities.

> *The Internet is the international job seeker's best friend. It opens up a whole new world of global job opportunities.*

The End of Mystery

The Internet is the international job seeker's best friend simply because it eliminates many of the traditional communication problems facing job seekers in this arena. Unlike the typical job search that takes place in a single community and involves frequent face-to-face communications between job seekers and employers, the international job search has always been a long-distance communication challenge.

Savvy international job seekers used to go about finding a job by locating key directories of international employers, contacting inter-national headhunters, surveying job listings, using personal contacts to network for information and referrals, or making trips abroad to locate potential employers. Their job search essentially involved sur-veying print publications, writing letters, mailing resumes, and using the telephone and fax. For many job seekers, the whole international job finding process was somewhat mysterious because of its long-distance nature and because of their inability to communicate with employers who might be interested in their skills and qualifications.

During the past 10 years, the Internet has gradually taken the mystery out of finding an international job. It also has provided a much needed structure to this arena. Through the use of email, search engines, and employment-oriented websites, you can literally conduct an international job search 24 hours a day in the quiet of your home or of-fice. Using key search engines and job boards, you can quickly identify em-ployers who are seeking individuals to work in thousands of locations around the world. By visiting employers' websites, you can acquire a great deal of "inside" information about the employer. Through job boards and employer websites, you can apply for many international jobs online. You

Through the use of email, search engines, and job boards, you can literally conduct an international job search 24 hours a day in the comfort of your home or office.

may even be interviewed online prior to actually meeting a potential employer for a face-to-face interview. In short, the Internet has become a wonderful communication medium that opens up what was once a relatively chaotic and disjointed international job market where efficient and effective long-distance communication was the key to uncovering opportunities.

The websites we identify speak for themselves: they put you in close contact with desirable jobs, employers, countries, and communi-ties. In the end, a few of the websites will become your favorite pathways for exploring a whole new world of job opportunities. You'll want to return to them again and again for information on employers, job vacancies, communities, and countries. This book, along with these websites, will literally become your best friend for navigating a world of job opportunities.

International Job Search

If you are like many other international job seekers, you love living and working in a multicultural world. It's an extremely rewarding experience which is often hard to explain to others. You meet interesting people, visit fascinating places, and enjoy a lifestyle that is difficult to find back home.

While the job search is often frustrating and disappointing, it also can be very educational, enlightening, and exhilarating. Indeed, the whole job search process will tell you a great deal about yourself and potential employers and future career opportunities. It may take three to six months to land an international job which may or may not be right for you. And then you may discover you made the wrong decision by accepting a position that is not a good fit. But your international job search will be extremely rewarding if you approach it with the right attitude, strategies, and resources to make your next career move a perfect fit for your interests, skills, and abilities. That's our mission in this guide to international jobs – make sure you are equipped with the best strategies and resources to make things happen for you. Hopefully, your attitude, which needs to be both positive and persistent despite disappointments, will serve you well as you embark on a great job search adventure to land an exciting new international job with a company or organization that will enable you to contribute and grow in the process of utilizing your unique talents.

Take Time and Do First Things First

So what do you want to do with the next stage of your life? Where do you want to live and work? Who may be most interested in your interests and talents?

In the following pages we outline numerous resources that should help you answer these and many other career-related questions. While you will have no problem finding a job, finding a job that you really love – one you do well and enjoy doing – will be your real challenge in the days and weeks ahead. Trust us when we tell you to take your time. Do first things first, which involves assessing your interests, skills, and abilities and then developing a clear career and job objective **before** writing your resume and contacting potential employers. For in the end, individuals who have a clear understanding of where they are coming from and where they want to go in the future will be best equipped to conduct a successful job search – one that results in a job they really love and which is on a career path that leads to a great deal of career satisfaction.

Timely International Resources

In addition to the many online resources identified in this book, we invite you to visit Impact Publications's websites for one of the Internet's largest collections of timely job search, international, and travel resources. The main website also includes the latest edition of their comprehensive *Work, Study, and Travel Abroad* catalog, which can be downloaded from the front page:

www.impactpublications.com

This site also includes numerous international employment and travel books in both paper and electronic (eBook) formats. You also can request a hard copy of the catalog by mail, phone, fax, or email:

> IMPACT PUBLICATIONS
> ATTN: International Jobs Catalog
> 9104 Manassas Drive, Suite N
> Manassas Park, VA 20111-5211 USA
> Tel. 703-361-7300 or Fax 703-335-9486
> Email: info@impactpublications.com

Their other sites include job- and travel-related resources, information, and advice:

- **WinningTheJob** winningthejob.com
- **ContentForCareers** contentforcareers.com
- **ContentForTravel** contentfortravel.com
- **iShopAroundTheWorld** shoparoundtheworld.com

Internet Employment Resources

For detailed information on using the Internet for conducting a job search, including all of the steps identified in Chapter 2, see two companion volumes on this subject:

Ron and Caryl Krannich, *America's Top Internet Job Sites* (Impact Publications, 2002)

Bernard Haldane Associates, *Haldane's Best Employment Websites for Professionals* (Impact Publications, 2002)

These and many other resources are listed at the end of this book. They also are available through the publisher's online career bookstore: impactpublications.com.

2

Organize an Effective Job Search

CONDUCTING AN INTERNATIONAL JOB SEARCH IS very similar to conducting a job search in general. If you are interested in finding a job that is right for you – one you do well and enjoy doing – your job search should follow several distinct steps.

Seven Job Search Steps

We recommend following these seven steps in sequence – do first things first – rather than jump around from one to another:

1. **Assess your interests, skills, and abilities:** This is the critical first step to conducting an effective job search. It involves assessing your interests, skills, values, motivations, and temperament based upon an analysis of your accomplishments. In other words, you need to identify your major strengths – what you do well and enjoy doing. Once you do this, you should be able to specify your motivated abilities and skills (MAS) which

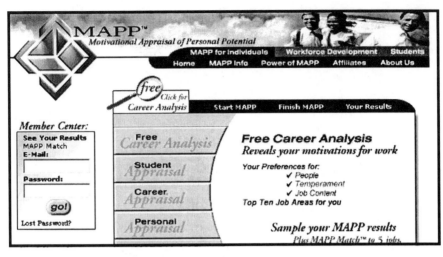

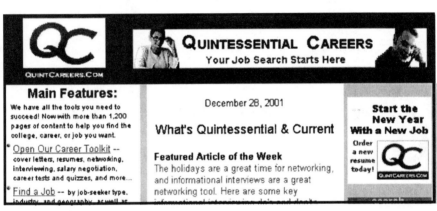

Main Features:

We have all the tools you need to succeed! Now with more than 1,200 pages of content to help you find the college, career, or job you want.

- Open Our Career Toolkit -- cover letters, resumes, networking, interviewing, salary negotiation, career tests and quizzes, and more...

- Find a Job -- by job-seeker type, industry, and geography, as well as

December 28, 2001

What's Quintessential & Current

Featured Article of the Week

The holidays are a great time for networking, and informational interviews are a great networking tool. Here are some key informational interviewing do's and don'ts

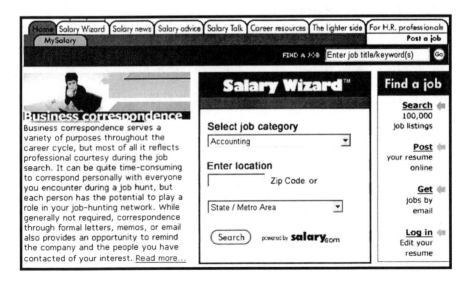

Business correspondence

Business correspondence serves a variety of purposes throughout the career cycle, but most of all it reflects professional courtesy during the job search. It can be quite time-consuming to correspond personally with everyone you encounter during a job hunt, but each person has the potential to play a role in your job-hunting network. While generally not required, correspondence through formal letters, memos, or email also provides an opportunity to remind the company and the people you have contacted of your interest. Read more...

Salary Wizard™

Select job category

Accounting

Enter location

Zip Code or

State / Metro Area

Search   powered by **salary**.com

Find a job

Search
100,000 job listings

Post
your resume online

Get
jobs by email

Log in
Edit your resume

Home | Salary Wizard | Salary news | Salary advice | Salary Talk | Career resources | The lighter side | For H.R. professionals

MySalary   Post a job

FIND A JOB Enter job title/keyword(s)   Go

are the basis for identifying and communicating your pattern of accomplishments on your resume and in interviews. For information on how to best complete this step, see the assessment chapters in our *Discover the Best Jobs for You* (Impact Publications) as well as visit the assessment websites noted on pages 18-19, such as assessment.com and careerhub.org. An example of motivated abilities and skills or a pattern of accomplishments for someone interested in working with an international nonprofit organization might be:

> Enjoy raising funds and organizing community development projects involving the participation of international donors, local officials, and community organizations. Consistently produce results that strengthen community decision-making.

2. **Specify your job and career objective:** This is essentially a paper and pencil exercise based on the assessment of your interests, skills, and abilities that has been formulated into a pattern of motivated skills and abilities. It should be a very succinct 20-40 word employer-centered statement of what it is you would like to accomplish in your next job that would benefit the employer. This may be the single most difficult activity to complete. Indeed, some job seekers may take two weeks of constantly refining their objective. Once completed, this objective will give important direction to your job search so you can target specific employers. Formulated properly, this objective will help you clearly communicate to employers exactly what it is you want to do for them. Without an objective, you may wander aimlessly from one interesting job description to another, rewrite your resume for each potential employer, and generally communicate that you're really not sure what you want other than to land a job which you hope you will enjoy. Whatever you do, don't make this mistake of trying to fit yourself into a job because you failed to complete this critical step in your job search. An international job objective targeted toward an international nonprofit organization might be stated as follows:

An increasingly responsible consulting position with an international nonprofit organization, where proven fund raising, community development leadership, and decision-making skills will be used to achieve the organization's decentralization mission.

3. **Conduct research on alternative opportunities:** Since you need to know who is hiring where for what types of jobs, you need to conduct a great deal of research on jobs, employers, organizations, and communities. Much of this research can be conducted via the Internet. Most communities and organizations have their own websites. To identify relevant communities and employers, use these major search engines which tend to yield the best results:

- google.com
- about.com
- iwon.com
- northernlight.com
- hotbot.com
- altavista.com

You may also want to use several other search engines that simultaneously encompass several other search engines:

- gogettem.com
- bjorgul.com
- queryserver.com
- vivisimo.com
- searchiq.com

For exploring job alternatives, check out the U.S. Department of Labor's website, especially its online version of the *Occupational Outlook Handbook*:

http://stats.bls.gov./ocohome.htm

For exploring job opportunities, visit several of these major online employment sites which include thousands of job listings:

- monster.com
- careerbuilder.com
- nationjob.com
- vault.com
- virtualresume.com
- headhunter.net

- flipdog.com
- hotjobs.com
- ajb.com
- careerweb.com

You'll also need to do research by using your local library and through networking and informational interviews. While research is always an ongoing process in any job search, your initial week or two of intensive research should yield very useful information for directing other stages of your job search. Visit the following sites for conducting research on a variety of occupational fields, professional associations, and employers:

- **Riley Guide**   rileyguide.com
- **Hoover's Online**   hoovers.com
- **Association on the Net**   ipl.org/ref/AON
- **AssociationCentral.com**   www.associationcentral.com
- **American Society of
  Association Executives**   www.asaenet.org
- **Quintessential Careers**   quintcareers.com
- **JobFactory**   jobfactory.com
- **Job Search Engine**   job-search-engine.com

Most libraries will have the following key directories for identifying thousands of professional and trade associations which can be critical to any job search:

> *Encyclopedia of Associations* (Thomson Learning)
> *National Trade and Professional Associations*
>   (Columbia Books)

4. **Write and distribute powerful attention-grabbing resumes and letters:** Once you've completed Steps 1, 2, and 3, you should be in an excellent position to write an outstanding resume as well as produce many different types of job search letters, including the ubiquitous cover letter that normally accompanies the resume. Since you've already completed an assessment, formulated an objective, and know your pattern of accomplishments, your resume should clearly reflect what you do well and enjoy doing – your motivated abilities and skills.

It should specially communicate what you have done, can do, and what you will do for the employer. In other words, it gives the employer strong evidence that you have a predictable pattern of performance because the content of your resume focuses on your pattern of accomplishments. As for letters, you should be prepared to write a series of job search letters that open the doors to key networking contacts and employers. These letters come in many different forms, including approach, cover, thank you, follow-up, and special letters. The most powerful letter you may ever write, one that can easily substitute for a resume, is the "T" letter. This letter focuses your qualifications and accomplishments, in a "T" format, around the specific requirements of a position. The following books are excellent resources for writing, producing, distributing, and following up the types of resumes and letters you should be using:

> *201 Dynamite Job Search Letters* (Ron and Caryl Krannich)
> *Cover Letters for Dummies* (Joyce Lain Kennedy)
> *Haldane's Best Resumes for Professionals* (Bernard Haldane Associates)
> *Haldane's Best Cover Letters for Professionals* (Bernard Haldane Associates)
> *High Impact Resume and Letters* (Ron Krannich and William Banis)
> *Resumes for Dummies* (Joyce Lain Kennedy)
> *The Savvy Resume Writer* (Ron and Caryl Krannich)

For information on the cultural nuances of resumes in over 40 different countries, including local employment contact information, see Mary Anne Thompson's international job search guide – *The Global Resume and CV Guide* – and website: www.goinglobal.com. For excellent examples of international resumes developed by professional resume writers who regularly work with international clients, see *Best Resumes and CVs for International Jobs* (Ron Krannich and Wendy Enelow). Several websites specialize in writing and distributing resumes.

If you want to work with a professional resume writer, contact the following companies and associations to locate a professional resume writer nearest you:

- **Advanced Career Systems** www.resumesystems.com
- **E-Resume.net** e-resume.net
- **Quintessential Careers** resumesandcoverletters. com
- **National Career Networking Association** ncna.com/cert.html
- **National Resume Writers' Association** nrwa.com
- **Professional Resumes Writing Association** www.prwra.com
- **Career Management Institute** cminstitute.com

Some websites specialize in "blasting" resumes to hundreds of key employers and headhunters. If you don't mind the expense and want to take a chance on such ostensibly quick and easy distribution methods, try these resume distribution websites:

- **ResumeSubmit** www.careerxpress.com
- **ResumeBlaster** resumeblaster.com
- **Resume Zapper** resumezapper.com
- **Blast My Resume** blastmyresume.com
- **CareerPal** careerpal.com

5. **Network and conduct informational interviews**: Networking still remains the most effective way of landing quality jobs. While you can spend a great deal of time going through newspapers, trade journals, newsletters, and online employment sites to identify and respond to job vacancies, the best quality jobs are found on what career counselors call the "hidden job market" – jobs that are not publicly announced but which are identified through interpersonal networking. This is especially true in the case of the international job arena. Many international jobs are acquired through personal contacts and word-of-

mouth communications. Consequently, it's incumbent upon you to initiate an effective networking campaign through which you conduct numerous informational interviews. These interviews are designed to generate a great deal of information, advice, and referrals that further build and expand your network of employment contacts. If done properly, your networking campaign will open many doors to job opportunities you might never have learned about had you only focused your job search on the advertised job market of published job vacancy announcements. For information on how to initiate such a campaign, including examples of the informational or referral interview, check out these four books:

> *A Foot in the Door* (Katharine Hansen)
> *Haldane's Best Answers to Tough Interview Questions*
>   (Bernard Haldane Associates)
> *Information Interviewing* (Martha Stoodley)
> *The Savvy Networker* (Ron and Caryl Krannich)

While many employment websites enable visitors to network through the use of community forums or bulletin boards, and many of the Usenet newsgroups and mailing lists function as centers for networking, a few websites are primarily designed for networking:

- **Advancing Women**   advancingwomen.com
- **HER Mail**   HERmail.net
- **Ask the Employer**   asktheemployer.com

6. **Interview for jobs**: The major purpose of all previous job search activities, including networking, resumes, and letters, is to get job interviews which hopefully will turn into job offers. If you've done your homework, you should be well prepared to handle the job interview. Again, keep in mind that employers want to know what **value** you will add or **benefits** you will bring to their organization. At this stage, they know you are probably technically qualified for the position. What they really want to know is whether you will fit well into their

organization. Consequently, they will be checking out your personality, social skills, and ability to take initiative and think on your feet. They may conduct a series of interviews as well as ask you behavioral questions. The key to managing this interview is preparation, preparation, and preparation. Study the interview situation; learn as much as possible about the employer; practice answering possible questions you will be asked; prepare yourself for *"what if"* or *"what did you, or would you, do in a case where . . ."* open-ended behavioral questions; and focus on telling short (1-3 minute) stories which would serve as examples to support your accomplishments. And be sure to ask questions about the job, the employer, and your future in the organization. Several excellent resources can help you prepare for this critical interview stage:

> *101 Dynamite Questions to Ask at Your Job Interview*
> (Richard Fein)
> *Haldane's Best Answers to Tough Interview Questions*
> (Bernard Haldane Associates)
> *Interview for Success* (Caryl and Ron Krannich)
> *Job Interviews for Dummies* (Joyce Lain Kennedy)
> *Proof of Performance* (Rick Nelles)

7. **Negotiate salary and benefits:** What exactly are you worth in today's job market? Are you usually paid what you are really worth, or don't you know for sure? Unfortunately, many people are underpaid because they (1) don't know what they are worth, and (2) fail to negotiate compensation. Indeed, many people take whatever they are offered. Some rationalize low pay and inequities by saying the money is not important to them. While that may be true, most people still want to be paid what they are worth. After all, money is one way of "keeping score" as to one's true value in the world of work. With more money, you can do more things that are important to you. If you've worked in government, you know your salary and benefits are predetermined by your official "grade" and "step." If you decide to work for a nonprofit organization, chances are you will be making 30 percent less than what you

can make in the private sector or even in government. Many nonprofits are on a fragile financial footing and thus have very little flexibility when it comes to negotiating compensation. Other nonprofits have more flexibility to negotiate salary and benefits than you may think. In any case, you should be prepared to negotiate compensation. Your focus should be on the value of the position – not solely on your previous compensation history. Your research should indicate the comparable value of positions as well as your own worth given your skills and experience. Several books can assist you in developing the necessary salary negotiation skills:

101 Ways to Improve Your Salary (Daniel Porot)
Better Than Money (David E. Gumpert)
Dynamite Salary Negotiations (Ron and Caryl Krannich)
Get More Money on the Next Job (Lee E. Miller)
Haldane's Best Salary Tips for Professionals (Bernard Haldane Associates)

Several excellent websites provide useful salary information to help individuals determine their market value. Be sure to visit these sites before you talk about compensation to an employer:

■ **Salary.com**	salary.com
■ **SalaryExpert**	salaryexpert.com
■ **JobStar**	jobstar.org
■ **WageWeb**	www.wageweb.com
■ **SalarySource**	salarysource.com

Employers' Expectations

One of the biggest mistakes job seekers make is to start their job search by writing a resume – the fourth step in a well organized and effective job search. Whatever you do, don't write your resume before following the first three steps in this seven step process. Take a week or two to complete the first few steps which will prepare you for writing a powerful resume that clearly communicates what employers want to know about candidates:

- What you have done in the past – your pattern of accomplishments

- What you can do at present – your current skill level

- What you will do in the future – your predictable performance

Always keep in mind what employers are looking for in candidates today:

predictable patterns of performance

Education and experience may be indicators of future performance, but employers want to know **what it is you will do for them in the future**. They are more interested in predicting your future performance in their organization than in learning about your past work history, education, activities, and awards. If, for example, you are a former Peace Corps Volunteer, most employers would not be interested in learning about your great latrine or weir project in village X of country Y. Instead, they would like to know if you have a **consistent pattern** of taking initiative, organizing projects, and providing key leadership in achieving goals, regardless of where such behavior takes place. Indeed, many employers may have little interest in your specific experience, other than as an indicator of your possible future performance, if indeed they can find a **pattern of accomplishments** arising out of that experience. Your job is to rise above discrete work activities in communicating your pattern of accomplishments so the employer can more easily predict your possible future performance. You do this by first understanding yourself – analyze who you really are in terms of a pattern of accomplishments. Once you understand this pattern, you need to communicate it to employers who are looking for evidence of such patterns rather than verbal promises of future

> *Employers are more interested in predicting your future performance than in learning about your past work history, education, activities, and awards.*

performance. In other words, you need to show them solid proof that you have a predictable pattern of behavior that will meet or exceed the employer's expectations.

Online Assessment Tools

Assessment is the key to organizing and conducting an effective job search. Several resources are available to assist you with this critical first step. If you've not taken the *Myers-Briggs Type Indicator*™, *Strong Interest Inventory*, or *Self-Directed Search* – the three most widely used assessment devices in career counseling – you should do so immediately. The results of these tests should be quite revealing for you in terms of communicating your interests, skills, and abilities to potential employers on resumes, in letters, and during interviews. These tests are widely available through community colleges and professional career counselors. You can even take these and several other relevant assessment tests online by visiting these useful websites:

- **Myers-Briggs Type Indicator**™ and **Strong Interest Inventory**   careerhub.org
- **Self-Directed Search**   self-directed-search.com
- **CareerLab.com**   careerlab.com
- **Personality Online**   spods.net/personality
- **MAPP**   assessment.com
- **Personality Type**   personalitytype.com
- **Analyze My Career**   analyzemycareer.com
- **Enneagram**   ennea.com
- **Career Services Group**   careerperfect.com
- **Collegeboard.com**   myroad.com
- **Career911**   12.32.113.198
- **OnlineProfiles**   onlineprofiles.com
- **QueenDom**   queendom.com
- **Personality and IQ Tests**   www.davideck.com
- **Tests on the Web**   2h.com
- **QuizBox**   www.quizbox.com
- **Fortune.com**   fortune.com/careers
- **Profiler**   profiler.com

- CareerLeader™   www.careerdiscovery.com/
                                    careerleader
- Careers By Design®   careers-by-design.com
- The Career Key   ncsu.edu/careerkey
- Futurestep   futurestep.com
- Jackson Vocational
  Interest Survey   jvis.com

Career Professionals

If you need a professional career counselor or career coach to assist you with the job search process, contact the following organizations that can refer you to such professionals:

- National Board of Certified
  Counselors, Inc.   nbcc.org
- National Career
  Development Association   ncda.org
- Certified Career Coaches   certifiedcareer.coaches.com
- Career Planning and Adult
  Development Network   careernetwork.org

If you need assistance in writing a resume, contact the following organizations which maintain lists of professional resume writers:

- Professional Association
  of Resume Writers and
  Career Coaches   www,parw.com
- Professional Resume
  Writing and Research
  Association   prwra.com
- National Resume
  Writers' Association   nrwa.com
- NetWorker Career Services   careercatalyst.com/resume.
                                    htm
- Career Masters Institute   cminstitute.com

3

Use Key Internet Resources

DURING THE PAST DECADE, THE INTERNET HAS INcreasingly played an important role in the employment process. Today more and more employers turn to the Internet to recruit candidates through their own home pages or by using online employment sites and databases. At the same time, more and more job seekers are including an Internet component in their job search.

Internet Employment Activities

Most individuals who use the Internet in their job search usually engage in four major activities:

1. Post resumes into online resume databases that are accessed by employers.

2. Survey job vacancies posted on home pages and through employment sites.

21

3. Conduct research on employers, compensation, and communities.

4. Network for information, advice, and referrals.

Knowing how to use search engines and email are the key skills for becoming an effective online job seeker. Learning such skills only takes a couple of hours. In fact, if you lack Internet skills, or need to brush up on using the Internet, you are well advised to get a copy of Angus J. Kennedy's *The Rough Guide to the Internet 2002*. This 528-page book offers a wealth of information and tips, including a directory of 2,000 sites, to assist both novices and seasoned users of the Internet.

For international job seekers, the Internet is a wonderful medium for locating employers and conducting a long-distance job search via email. Indeed, a potential employer in Sydney or Capetown will most likely want you to email a copy of your resume, along with an accompanying cover letter, as well as conduct a screening interview online.

Being volatile businesses, only one third of all current websites may be functioning within the next two years.

Using the Internet to conduct an international job search is relatively easy once you start using key search engines and locate a few major websites that provide linkages to the international employment community. In the following sections we identify several websites that can be useful in conducting an international job search. However, please be forewarned that some of these sites may go out of business and disappear altogether or merge with other websites in the coming months and years. Indeed, only one third of all current websites will probably be functioning within the next two years (2004). Therefore, it is incumbent upon you to identify new websites that can assist you with your international job search.

Online Job Search Resources

If you are new to using the Internet for conducting a job search, you are well advised to consult several of the following books that provide

details on using the Internet for finding a job. Several of these resources go through the whole process of using the Internet for conducting employment research, posting resumes, and communicating
by email. Others primarily annotate the best sites on the Internet:

100 Top Internet Job Sites (Kristina M. Ackley)

Adams Internet Job Search Almanac (Michelle Roy Kelly, ed.)

America's Top Internet Job Sites (Ron and Caryl Krannich)

CareerXroads 2002 (Gerry Crispin and Mark Mehler)

Career Exploration on the Internet (Ferguson Publishing)

Cyberspace Job Search Kit (Fred E. Jandt and Mary B. Nemnich)

The Everything Online Job Search Book (Steve Graber)

The Guide to Internet Job Searching (Margaret Riley Dikel and
Frances E. Roehm)

Haldane's Best Employment Websites for Professionals
(Bernard Haldane Associates)

Job-Hunting on the Internet (Richard Nelson Bolles)

Job Searching Online For Dummies, With CD-ROM (Pam Dixon)

Sams Teach Yourself e-Job Hunting Today (Eric Schlesinger
and Susan Musich)

Weddle's Job-Seeker's Guide to Employment Web Sites
(Peter D. Weddle)

Most of these books are available in libraries and bookstores or they
can be ordered directly from Impact Publications (see order form at
the end of this book or visit impactpublications.com).

Search Engines, Agents, and Directories

You will literally find hundreds of search engines designed to assist Internet users in finding information efficiently and effectively. A few websites regularly rank the most popular employment websites and search engines on the Internet:

- **Ranks**   ranks.com/hom/lifestyle/top_
                               job_search_sites
- **100Hot**   100hot.com/list.gsp?category=
                               business&keywords=jobs
- **Search Engine Watch**   searchenginewatch.com/links

Actually, the process of searching for information on the Internet is organized by three types of search mechanisms:

- Search engines
- Search agents
- Directories

Search engines use "spiders" that crawl the Internet in search of keywords, phrases, and other information you specify as part of your search. **Search agents**, also known as searchbots, operate like search engines but they also search the various search engines in compiling more information than a single search engine. **Directories** are compilations of websites organized under a single subject, such as "Employment," "Travel," and "Cities."

If you decide to use search engines in your online job search, we recommend that you start with the always reliable, no-nonsense, and unadorned **Google.com**:

google.com

Other individual key search engines to use include:

- **iWon**   iwon.com
- **Overture**   overture.com
- **Northern Light**   northernlight.com

- HotBot   hotbot.com
- AltaVista   altavista.com
- AOL Anywhere   search.aol.com
- C4.com   c4.com
- CEO Express   ceoexpress.com
- Debriefing   debriefing.com
- Direct Hit   directhit.com
- EuroSeek   euroseek.com
- Excite   excite.com
- FAST Search   alltheweb.com
- Go/InfoSeek   go.com
- inFind   infind.com
- Looksmart   looksmart.com
- Lycos   lycos.com
- Microsoft Network   msn.com
- NBCi   nbci.com
- Netscape   netscape.com
- Raging Search   raging.com
- Searchbeat   searchbeat.com
- Webcrawler   webcrawler.com
- Yahoo   yahoo.com

If you want to use several of these search engines at the same time, check out these multiple and meta search engines:

- GoGettem   gogettem.com
- ixquick   ixquick.com
- 1-Page Multi Search   bjorgul.com
- QueryServer   queryserver.com
- Search IQ   searchiq.com
- Vivisimo   vivisimo.com

Some of the most popular **search agents**, which simultaneously search a limited number (5-15) of search engines and directories, include the following:

- Ask Jeeves   ask.com
- DogPile   dogpile.com

- Go2Net   go2net.com
- InfoZoid   infozoid.com
- Mamma   mamma.com
- MetaCrawler   metacrawler.com
- MetaGopher   metagopher.com
- Monster Crawler   monstercrawler.com
- RedeSearch   redesearch.com
- Search.com   search.com
- ProFusion   profusion.com

Search.com also includes an international meta search engine for conducting searches in specific countries:

search.com/search?channel=15

Some of the most useful websites that primarily function as **directories** include the following:

- About.com   about.com
- Ask Jeeves   ask.com
- Britannica   britannica.com
- DogPile   dogpile.com
- Excite   excite.com
- Go   go.com
- iWon   iwon.com
- Looksmart   looksmart.com
- Lycos   lycos.com
- Microsoft Network   msn.com
- Netscape   netscape.com
- Open Directory   dmoz.org
- Yahoo   yahoo.com

Virtual Communities for Networking

The Internet is made up of thousands of loosely structured communities of individuals variously called Usenet newsgroups, mailing lists, and message boards. Individuals with common interests form, join, or participate in these groups for a variety of reasons. Many of these groups are useful arenas for acquiring information, advice, and referrals – places to network with fellow members. You may want to check out many of these groups to see if some may be useful to your job search. In fact, you may want to form your own group which could function as a network for acquiring information and advice useful for conducting an international job search.

Since there are over 40,000 Usenet newsgroups on the Internet, you will need a search engine to locate the ones most related to your interests. The following sites will help you sort through the maze of newsgroups:

- **CareerKey** careerkey.com/newsgroups.htm
- **Cyberfiber** www.cyberfiber.com
- **JobBankUSA** jobbankusa.com/usejobs.html
- **Google** groups.google.com
- **Topica** topica.com
- **Usenet Info Center** metalab.unc.edu/usenet-i/home.html
- **Questions** xs4all.nl/~wijnands/nnq/

A good source for identifying newsgroups relevant to conducting a job search in the United States, Canada, and a few other countries and regions (Australia, Bermuda, Denmark, Europe, Ireland, Israel, Ukraine, United Kingdom, and South Africa) is Career Internetworking:

www.careerkey.com/newsgroups.htm

Mailing lists tend to be less spontaneous than newsgroups. You usually subscribe to these groups which are normally moderated by someone who created the list. Until you decide to "unsubscribe" to the list, you will regularly receive email, either individually or in digest format, of ongoing discussions. For a directory of more than 7,500 mailing lists, visit this site:

http://paml.net

If, for example, you are interested in subscribing to lists for specific countries or regions, you can search by keyword to find an appropriate list. For Costa Rica and Italy, go to these sites:

- **Costa Rica**   egroups.com/list/Costa_Rica
- **Italy**   topica.com/dir/?cid=705

The following sites provide access to tens of thousands of mailing lists:

- **Yahoo! Groups**   groups.yahoo.com
- **Topica**   topica.com
- **Coollist**   coollist.com

In addition to identifying and becoming a member of various mailing lists, each of these sites provides information on how you can create your own free mailing list.

Major Employment Websites

Employment websites have grown by leaps and bounds over the past few years. Today more than 100,000 employment sites function on the Internet. Many of these sites provide a comprehensive collection of employment services relevant to job seekers: job postings, resume databases, employer profiles, job news, career articles and advice, and message boards. While you should visit several of these sites for information and advice, be sure to survey their job listings as well as post your resume online. Some sites, such as Monster.com, include a large international jobs section as well as a special hosted message board ("Work Abroad") for international job seekers:

http://forums.monstercom/forum.asp?forum=119

Be sure to survey Monster's job listings as well as review the questions and answers on the message board. You may want to post your own questions in order to get useful information and advice.

Finding which sites are most appropriate for your interests can be a daunting task. While most sites are primarily focused on jobs in North America, several of these sites also include international jobs.

Many of those jobs are disproportionately in the fields of sales, marketing, and finance. Sites such as Monster.com also have affiliate sites in major cities around the world. The major online employment sites include:

▪ Monster.com	monster.com
▪ Direct Employers	directemployers.com
▪ America's Job Bank	www.ajb.dni.us
▪ CareerBuilder	careerbuilder.com
▪ NationJob	nationjob.com
▪ FlipDog	flipdog.com
▪ Hot Jobs	hotjobs.com
▪ Headhunter.net	headhunter.net
▪ Jobs.com	jobs.com
▪ Jobsonline	jobsonline.com
▪ CareerJournal	careerjournal.com
▪ CareerFlex	careerflex.com
▪ Employment911.com	employment911.com
▪ EmploymentSpot	employmentspot.com
▪ JobFactory	jobfactory.com
▪ Job Sniper	jobsniper.com
▪ Vault.com	vault.com
▪ WebFeet.com	webfeet.com
▪ MyJobSearch	myjobsearch.com
▪ PlanetRecruit	planetrecruit.com
▪ 4Work	4work.com
▪ BestJobsUSA	bestjobsusa.com
▪ BrilliantPeople.com	brilliantpeople.com
▪ Career Shop	careershop.com
▪ Job Sleuth	jobsleuth.com
▪ Career City	careercity.com
▪ JobOptions	joboptions.com
▪ JobTrak	jobtrak.com
▪ JobOpps.net	jobopps.net
▪ Brass Ring	brassring.com
▪ Career.com	career.com
▪ JobBankUSA	jobbankusa.com
▪ Net-Temps	net-temps.com

- CareerTV   careertv.net
- Jumbo Classifieds   jumboclassifieds.com
- Preferred Jobs   preferredjobs.com
- JobOpps.net   jobopps.net
- ProHire   prohire.com
- CareerExchange   careerexchange.com
- Career Magazine   careermag.com
- Employers Online   employersonline.com
- EmployMax   employmax.com
- CareerWeb   careerweb.com
- WantedJobs   wantedjobs.com
- JobFactory   jobfactory.com
- MindFind   mindfind.com
- JobExchange   employmentwizard.com
- RecruitUSA   recruitusa.com
- Recruiters Online Network   recruitersonline.com
- kForce.com   kforce.com
- Dice.com   dice.com
- Washington Post   washingtonjobs.com

Online International Communities

Several websites attract numerous international job seekers who have similar community interests. The following sites are well worth exploring for information, advice, contacts, and linkages to other international employment sites:

- iAgora.com   iagora.com
- Transitions Abroad   transitionsabroad.com
- Escape Artist   escapeartist.com
- Teaching Jobs Overseas   joyjobs.com

Content of Employment Websites

Most employment websites have a very similar structure and purpose. Over 80 percent of all employment websites function as job boards with separate sections for job seekers and employers. As such, they usually include two key components:

1. Job postings
2. Resume database and/or job alerts

Some sites include a job alert section in lieu of a resume database. This allows job seekers to automatically receive by email any new job postings that meet their specific interest criteria. Most sites are free to job seekers. Employers pay various user fees to post jobs and search resume databases.

Many employment websites include some combination of the following services designed to attract repeat traffic to their sites:

- Job Search Tips
- Featured Articles
- Career Experts or Advisors
- Career Tool Kit
- Career Assessment Tests
- Community Forums
- Discussion or Chat Groups
- Message Boards
- Job Alert ("Push") Emails
- Company Research Centers
- Networking Forums
- Salary Calculators or Wizards
- Resume Management Center
- Resume and Cover Letter Advice
- Multimedia Resume Software
- Job Interview Practice
- Relocation Information
- Reference Check Checkers
- Employment or Career News
- Free Email For Privacy
- Success Stories
- Career Newsletter
- Career Events
- Online Job Fairs
- Affiliate Sites
- Career Resources
- Featured Employers

- Polls and Surveys
- Contests
- Online Education and Training
- International Employment
- Talent Auction Centers
- Company Ads (buttons and banners)
- Sponsored Links
- Special Channels for Students, Executives, Freelancers, Military, and other groups

Huge mega employment sites such as Monster.com include over 80 percent of these add-on services. Most sites, however, are very basic in their orientation – primarily include job postings and resume data-bases and maybe a newsletter designed to capture emails of job seekers who must register in order to receive the newsletter.

4

International Executive Recruiters

I F YOU EXPECT TO EARN IN EXCESS OF $75,000 A YEAR, you are well advised to include headhunters, executive recruiters, and executive search firms in your job search. These individuals and groups primarily work for employers who pay them 25 to 35 percent of a candidate's first-year salary for a successful placement.

Headhunters and executive search firms focus on recruiting qualified individuals to fill upper-level positions in companies. If you qualify for such positions, you should contact several international executive search firms that specialize in your particular skills and level of experience. Reach them by phone, fax, mail, or email in order to get your resume in their hands and database. Most headhunters and executive search firms welcome resumes from qualified candidates whom they can market to their clients.

The Hidden International Job Market

Many of the best paying and most challenging international job opportunities are never advertised to the public. In fact, many international employers prefer recruiting personnel through specialized executive

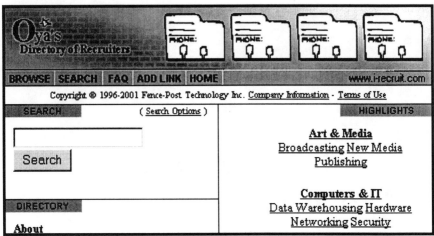

SEARCH (Search Options)

Search

DIRECTORY

About

HIGHLIGHTS

Art & Media
Broadcasting New Media
Publishing

Computers & IT
Data Warehousing Hardware
Networking Security

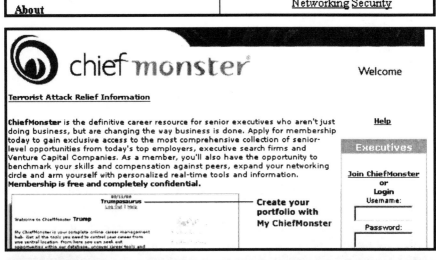

chief monster

Welcome

Terrorist Attack Relief Information

ChiefMonster is the definitive career resource for senior executives who aren't just doing business, but are changing the way business is done. Apply for membership today to gain exclusive access to the most comprehensive collection of senior-level opportunities from today's top employers, executive search firms and Venture Capital Companies. As a member, you'll also have the opportunity to benchmark your skills and compensation against peers, expand your networking circle and arm yourself with personalized real-time tools and information. **Membership is free and completely confidential.**

Help

Executives

Join ChiefMonster
or
Login
Username:

Password:

Create your portfolio with My ChiefMonster

BrilliantPeople.com
Powered by MRI

MRI Management Recruiters International, Inc.

Search for Jobs ►
Find a Recruiter ►
Manage Your Career ►

Career Helpers
My Resume
Ask a Recruiter
Career Resources

Skill Builders
Skill Assessment

Online Tools
Salary Wizard
Relocation Tools

The jobs. The recruiters. The good life.

My Jobs
☑ SEARCH FOR JOBS

All ▼
Keywords **Go►**

Using intelligent matching technology, you'll find the right job

My Recruiter
☑ FIND A RECRUITER

All ▼
Keywords **Go►**

Employers use MRI recruiters to find the best talent. MRI recruiters

My Career
☑ MANAGE YOUR CAREER

All ▼
Login | Sign Up **Go►**

Keep your career on track with resume builders, customized search agents and other recruiters or headhunters rather than advertise positions through newspapers, magazines, or online. These recruiters play an important role in locating qualified candidates – sometimes even raiding the competition's personnel – and screening them prior to presenting them as qualified candidates to be interviewed for positions. And the Internet has become the headhunter's best friend for locating talent through resume databases and job postings. Indeed, many of the job postings for $75,000+ jobs found on the major employment websites are actually sponsored by headhunters who seek to recruit qualified candidates to present to their clients.

> *Executive recruiters operate a "hidden job market" of international opportunities. If you earn more than $100,000 a year, it's imperative that you contact these recruiters.*

Since many executive-level positions are never advertised through traditional recruitment channels, executive recruiters literally operate a "hidden job market" where information on high-level vacancies is primarily found through contacts with these recruiters. Consequently, it is in your interest to get your resume in the hands of several recruiters who specialize in your area of international expertise. In fact, if you earn more than $100,000 a year, it's imperative that you include executive recruiters as key players in your job search. Chances are your next job opportunity will come via a headhunter rather than as a result of a direct application with an employer.

Identifying International Headhunters

Individuals with a great deal of professional work experience, as well as exotic, hard-to-find international skills, should contact international executive search firms. Also known as headhunters, these firms tend to specialize in particular occupational areas. They work for employers who hire and/or retain them to find employees to fill specific positions. Many of the job openings available through executive search firms are never advertised in print or electronic media. The most comprehensive directories of such firms are published annually by Kennedy Information (kennedyinfo.com):

❏ *Directory of Executive Search Firms:* Published annually, this is the "Red Book" bible for anyone using headhunters and executive search firms. Its nearly 1,200 pages list more than 14,000 executive recruiters at 8,110 offices who are identified by recruitment specialty, name, address, telephone, fax, and email. While primarily focusing on U.S.-based executive recruiters, it also includes firms in Canada and Mexico. The book comes complete with a CD-ROM that demos the company's SearchSelect® mail merge and mailing label program ($195) for targeting executive recruiters listed in the book with resumes and letters.

❏ *Kennedy's International Directory of Executive Recruiters:* Lists more than 2,500 executive recruiters associated with 1,087 firms in 59 countries. Includes full contact information (name, address, phone, fax, and email when available), detailed firm descriptions, and salary minimums.

Since most of the executive search firms listed in these two books regularly collect resumes for their databases, you should contact several of these firms by sending them a resume and letter indicating your international interests, skills, and experience. Kennedy Information also offers a special resume email service ($99.00) for targeting executive recruiters by special industry, function, geography, and salary range:

executiveagent.com

Both of the Kennedy Information books are available through Impact Publications (impactpublications.com and resource section at the end of this book).

Kennedy Information also conducts an annual survey of the largest international executive search firms. The results of the survey are published in their monthly newsletter *Executive Recruiter News*. A summary of the top 20 international retained search firms can be found on their website:

kennedyinfo.com/er/ern201w.html

You also can locate numerous executive search firms online by using the many search engines outlined in Chapter 3. However, one of the best one-stop online resources for locating such firms is Oya's Directory of Recruiters:

Oya's Directory of Recruiters   Executive Recruiters
i-recruit.com

This is one of the Internet's best sites for locating recruiters. Free to both job seekers and recruiters, this site's database includes thousands of recruiters classified into 14 major categories:

- Agriculture
- Art and Media
- Computers & IT
- Construction
- Education
- Engineering & Science
- Executive
- Finance
- Hospitality
- Industrial
- International
- Medical
- Professional
- Transportation

If you want to target recruiters in a particular professional field, search for them by specialty and send them your resume. Most recruiters welcome resumes by indicating the types of skill sets they need and including their email addresses and telephone and fax numbers. You also can search for recruiters by location, including international recruiters by specialty:

i-recruit.com/drecruiters_type_international.htm

A great site for exploring the "hidden job market" of recruiters.

You also may want to check out RecruitersCafe.com. This site allows users to locate search firms by agency name, geographic focus, and industry specialization.

A Web of Executive Recruiters

Several executive search firms also maintain websites. Other websites are designed for recruiting executive-level talent, especially individuals expecting to make in excess of $100,000 a year. With offices or affiliates worldwide, many of these firms function as international recruiters, headhunters, and professional staffing firms.

The following websites specialize in executive-level positions and executive recruiters. While many of them are free to job seekers, some charge monthly, quarterly, or yearly membership fees to use their online services. Some also sponsor recruitment events for networking with recruiters. The following websites, for example, charge job seekers membership fees for using their sites:

- ExecuNet   execunet.com
- ExecutivesOnly   executivesonly.com
- Netshare   netshare.com

On the other hand, these popular executive-level sites are free for job seekers:

- 6 Figure Jobs   sixfigurejobs.com
- Chief Monster.com   my.chief.monster.com
- Management Recruiters
  International   brilliantpeople.com
- Recruiters Online Network recruitersonline.com

Anyone planning to use executive recruiters in their job search should first explore these major executive recruiting sites:

Chief Monster.com   **Executive Recruiters**
  International
my.chief.monster.com

Operated by the largest online employment site – Monster.com – this relatively new specialty site is designed for senior executives who seek to contact top employers, executive search firms, and venture capital companies. Membership is required but free and confidential. Both job seekers and employers must join this site in order to use its many services. Job seekers must meet certain experience and salary qualifications in order to participate in the site. Includes a resume database, job listings, networking opportunities, and useful articles for job seekers. Before paying monthly membership fees to other executive recruiting sites, be sure to explore the free opportunities available through this Monster.com site. If it operates like the rest of Monster.com, it should offer some good opportunities for senior executives – and the price is right. The site allows users to develop their own portfolio online. Includes a wealth of useful online information and contacts. If you make over $125,000 a year, you should definitely become a member of this useful site.

Management Recruiters International brilliantpeople.com	Executive Recruiters

This site claims to represent the world's largest executive search and recruitment organization (Management Recruiters International) with more than 1,000 offices and 5,000 search professionals in North America, Europe, and Asia. Participation in this site puts you into MRI's recruitment system. The site includes a resume database, job postings, MRI recruiters, and an online resume editing and an application tracking system. It is part of a large workplace solutions company with $1.7 billion in annual billings (cdicorp.com). This site also includes useful career tools for assessing skills (entrinskik.net), improving resumes, and acquiring salary (salary.com) and relocation information (homefair.com). Its career resources section includes tips on resumes, interviews, career counselors, and working with a recruiter.

Recruiters Online Network   Executive Recruiters
recruitersonline.com

Job seekers can view job postings online as well as post their resumes on this site for free. Includes a section for locating recruiters and headhunters by industry (67 specialty areas) and location. Over 8,000 registered recruiters, executive search firms, employment agencies, and headhunters use this site. Employers and recruiters pay monthly fees for using this site, which also includes broadcasting their job postings to over 1,500 other websites.

6 FigureJobs   Executive Recruiters
sixfigurejobs.com

Designed for experienced professionals, this $100,000+ site invites executive-level candidates to post their resumes online as well as explore job postings of their client companies. You must become a member in order to use this site. However, unlike similar executive-level sites, membership for job seekers is free. Includes several useful career resources, such as a salary wizard (Salary.com), bookstore (Amazon.com), expert advice (Deltaroad.com), online learning (Thinq.com), resume services (Career-resumes.com), an executive newsletter, and recommended links. You also can research companies (Hoovers.com), explore relocation issues, locate recruiters, and ask questions. Special features include online seminars (powerhiring.com), job-related news, and success stories.

ExecutivesOnly   Executive Recruiters
executivesonly.com

Focusing on executives with an annual earnings potential of $70,000 to $750,000, this site includes numerous job postings by employers and recruiters. Its revenue model is very different from 99 percent of other employment-related websites. While most sites are supported by employers and recruiters and free to job seekers, this one is just the opposite – free to employers and recruiters but costs job seekers membership fees to use it: $145 for 14 weeks; $189 for 24 weeks; $259 for 36 weeks; and $389 for 48 weeks. The site also offers a premium resume service with a 14-week membership ($695) as well as several other fee-based services (consulting, interview mentor, and resume blasting at $1.95 per resume).

Netshare netshare.com	Executive Recruiters

This award-winning executive-level site is designed to connect executive job seekers ($100,000+) with companies and re-cruiters. Includes a resume database and nearly 2,000 executive job listings provided by executive recruiters and companies as well as special free services for job seekers (market intelligence, career coaching, resume critique, and Q&A). Individuals must register and pay monthly membership fees in order to use this site. These range from $125 for three months to $385 for 12 months, depending on the category of membership.

ExecuNet execunet.com	Executive Recruiters

Focusing on $100,000+ executive-level candidates, this popular site primarily offers job postings to potential candidates. This is a no-cost service to employers and recruiters who list posi-tions. Job seekers pay membership fees to access the services of this site: 3 months for $135; 6 months for $199; and 12 months for $349. Members receive a free resume review, access to the job database and hundreds of recruiters and companies, job search tips, research tools, a newsletter, and local network-ing opportunities. However, you can access the networking opportunities, which are primarily listings of upcoming break-fast meetings and cocktail parties sponsored by ExecuNet and many other organizations, without being a member. Nonmembers also can access other free sections of this site that deal with career resources or what they call "Knowledge." Like a few other membership sites that charge job seekers for proprietary online services, we have no idea as to the relative effectiveness of this site compared to sites, such as Chief Monster.com, 6FigureJobs, and Recruiters Online Network, that are free to job seekers.

Korn/Ferry International   Executive Recruiters
ekornferry.com

This is one of the world's largest and most respected executive search firms. Its website includes a sampling of executive career opportunities represented by Korn/Ferry International. These sample listings, which are very current, will give you a good idea of this company's recruitment activities. You can search for opportunities by region and job category. If you are seeking a senior-level international position, be sure to register on this site. In so doing, you can enter your resume and profile into their database, which they constantly search for candidates meeting their clients' hiring criteria.

Heidrick & Struggles   Executive Recruiters
heidrick.com

Operating since 1953, this large international executive recruitment and management firm has nearly 1,900 professionals in 75 offices around the world. The site allows you to contact a professional directly by industry expertise and location. You can upload your resume in ASCII format and send it directly to the professional. The company covers a wide range of sectors, from consumer, diversity, e-business, education, and nonprofits to financial services, health care, industrial, professional services, and technology.

Spencer Stuart · spencerstuart.com — Executive Recruiters

This is another one of world's largest and most respected executive search firms, which operates a network of 52 offices in 25 countries. This excellent website includes a wealth of information on the company and its services as well as useful job search tips and resources on salaries, self-assessment, and upcoming events and seminars. If you register as a member, you receive executive opportunities by email that match your particular interests, skills, and experience. The firm recruits and places candidates in 13 major practice areas: agribusiness, aviation, board services, consumer goods and services, diversity, energy and natural resources, financial services, industrial, Internet, life science, logistics and supply chain management, not-for-profit, and technology and communication.

The following companies offer a variety of executive search services. Some specialize in one or two occupational and industrial areas whereas others cover several areas. As you explore these firms and services, be sure they represent your area of international expertise.

- **Bartholdi & Company** — bartholdisearch.com
- **International Staffing Consultants** — iscworld.com
- **Contracts Consultancy Ltd.** — ccl.uk.com
- **Nicholson International** — nicholsonintl.com
- **PricewaterhouseCoopers** — pwcglobal.com
- **John Clements** — johnclements.com
- **Emds** — emdsnet.com
- **Egon Zehnder** — egonzehnder.com
- **Sheladia Associates** — sheladia.com
- **InterTech Services** — intertech.socp.com
- **HE International** — hei-inc.com
- **Ashtead Management Consultants** — ashteadman.co.uk

- Isaacson Miller Executive
  Search   execsearches.com
- Ronnie Boyd & Associates   boydhouston.com
- Hampton Recruitment
  Consultancy   hampton.co.za
- Headhunter.net   headhunter.net
- JDV International   jdvinternational.com
- Avotek Headhunters   avotek.nl
- Global Medical Staffing   gmedical.com
- M & M Staff Recruitment   mmstaff.co.uk

Resume Email Blasting Services

How can you quickly get international executive recruiters to take notice of your qualifications? Short of contacting each company individually via their website, email, mail, telephone, or fax, you may want to use the services of companies that specialize in distributing resumes en masse to executive recruiters. Indeed, one of the quickest ways to reach executive recruiters is to broadcast or blast your resume to such firms using resume blasting services. These companies specialize in emailing clients' resumes to thousands of headhunters who wish to receive free resumes from potential executive-level candidates.

You should approach resume blasting businesses as you would any direct-mail business – with caution. None of these firms guarantee the quality of their services

Many of these firms also include employers and job boards in their email distribution systems. The cost of using such firms to email your resume to 1,000 to 10,000 executive recruiters can range from $24 to over $4,000.

While many of these firms claim remarkable successes for their paying clients, you should approach these businesses as you would any direct-mail business – with caution. None of these firms guarantee the quality of their services. In fact, few resume broadcast firms reveal information about the structure and quality of their mailing lists. Therefore, before using any of these firms, it's in your interest to learn as much as possible about the international content of their lists. For example, what percentage of their resume recipients specialize in your area of expertise? How many employers versus executive recruiters and venture capital firms are included in their mailing list? What percentage are international recruitment firms? If they can't answer these three questions to your satisfaction, you may be wasting your money on a service that is high on expectations but low on performance. After all, many of these firms only deal with headhunters focused on recruiting candidates for employers in the U.S.

The following resume broadcasting firms primarily work with headhunters and executive search firms. All of them charge job seekers resume blasting fees:

- BlastMyResume — blastmyresume.com
- CareerPal — careerpal.com
- E-cv.com — e-cv.com
- Executiveagent.com — executiveagent.com
- HotResumes — hotresumes.com
  (posts to multiple job boards)
- Job Search Page — jobsearchpage.com
  (international focus)
- Job Village — jobvillage.com
  (Resume Agent) — (resumeagent.com)
  (Resumeshotgun) — (resumeshotgun.com)
- ResumeBlaster — resumeblaster.com
- Resume Booster — resumebooster.com
- ResumeBroadcaster — resumebroadcaster.com
- Resume Carpet Bomber — resumecarpetbomber.com
- Resume Path — resumepath.com
- ResumeSubmit — www.careerxpress.com
- ResumeZapper — resumezapper.com
- ResumeXpress — resumexpress.com
- RocketResume — rocketresume.com
- See Me Resumes — seemeresumes.com
- Your Missing Link — yourmissinglink.com
- WSACORP.com — www.wsacorp.com

Knowing how these services work, you may want to develop your own specialized email list of international executive recruiters. Such a list would be more targeted and you would maintain better control of the content of your communication for such firms.

5

Global and Expat Websites

S EVERAL WEBSITES OFFER A BROAD INTERNATIONAL
employment focus. Functioning as gateway sites to the international employment arena, they include a variety of services:
job postings, resume databases, employer profiles, contact
information, job search tips, relocation and expat information, cultural
insights, and resources for pursuing international jobs and lifestyles.
Designed for the individual job seeker, many of these sites are well
worth visiting in addition to executive recruiters and region- or
country-specific sites.

The websites featured in this chapter represent a diverse mix of
international-oriented employment sites. Each tends to take a different
approach to the global job market, from the advertising-driven
Monster.com international job board to the information-rich and
irreverent escapeartist.com.

Key Gateway Sites

The following websites include a wealth of information on international jobs, with many offering job listings, resume databases, career

EscaperArtist.com

✉ EMAIL

| HOME | OFFSHORE REAL ESTATE | OFFSHORE INVESTMENTS | EMBASSIES | JOBS OVERSEAS | LIVING OVERSEAS | COUNTRIES | MAGAZINE |

[Search]

Search By Country · Topic · or Subject · *Search Help*

☀ **C L I C K   H E R E**
Send This WebPage To A Friend

International Real Estate Marketplace Featured Listings

ESCAPE FROM AMERICA
MAGAZINE

Real Estate in Panama - Panama Canal Zone Properties

Isla Solarte Island Community Bocas Del Toro - Panama Lots: $25,000 - $55,000

Magnificent Heritage House With Income New Zealand US$328,000 OBO

Waterbreath Retreat Sunshine Coast Queensland Australia US$490,000

Get 9% Return On Investment Panama, Condo: $199,000 or $1,650 month

Guesthouse New 25% Revenue 90% Occupation Santo Domingo $260,000

View More Properties · List Your Property for FREE!

| **Living Overseas** | **Investing Offshore** |

Our Expatriate Magazine ·   Offshore Investments ·
Overseas Jobs ·   2nd Passports ·
Moving & Living Overseas ·   Tax Havens ·

OFFSHORE REAL ESTATE
QUARTERLY

A|RS | JOB BOARDS

Login | Become a Member

1-800-466-4010 | Request Info | Course Catalog | Schedule | Shopping Cart | My Passport

| HOME | NEWS | LIBRARY | FORUMS | JOB BOARDS | PRODUCTS | TOOLS | ABOUT AIRS |

The Largest Collection of Job Boards on the Web

Friday, December 23, 2001

Career Hubs   1006 Job Boards

National   Midwest
Northeast   Southwest
Northwest   Southwest

International   329 Job Boards

International   Central America
Africa   Europe
Asia   Middle East
Canada   South America
Caribbean   South Pacific

SEARCH

[   ] [Go ▶]

A Great Recruitment Job!
AIRS RecruiterJobs >>

Function   224 Job Boards

Admin & Support Services   Executive   HR & Recruiting
Customer Service   Finance & Accounting   Sales

POST
To 2,000 Job Boards!
AIRSPost >

Industry   893 Job Boards

Advertising, Marketing, PR   Engineering   Pharmaceutical
Agriculture & Forestry   Environmental   Property Mgmt/Facilities
Arts & Entertainment   Food & Beverage   Quality Assurance/Safety
Automotive   Government   Real Estate
Aviation & Aerospace   Hospitality & Travel   Retail

ADD
Your Job Board!
AIRS Job Board Directory >>

GOINGLOBAL

Grassroots Intelligence for Global Careers

▷ About Us
▷ Contact
▷ Home

Goinglobal.com's mission is to encourage, inform and support the international career seeker. Our unique content provides the user with a comprehensive tool kit of information and resources for evaluating, selecting, and transitioning into a successful career in a foreign country. Our team of in-country career experts are dedicated to providing the latest "grass roots intelligence" for the global career seeker.

Site Features
Country Profile
Custom Search
Buy A Guide
Hot Topics
Membership
Global Forum
Read Reviews

Country Profiles -
Goinglobal.com currently has career information for 23 countries throughout Europe, Asia, and the Americas. Click on "Country Profiles" to see what countries are included. Each country profile gives you an

Country Career Guides - If you like what you see on the Goinglobal.com site, you can purchase and download the complete career guide for the country of your choice. These extensive guides —many of them 75 pages or more— provide the latest advice, and linkages to other relevant websites. If you start your online international job search by visiting these four gateway sites, you may save yourself a great deal of job search time. Best of all, these sites will open up a whole new world of employment and international information within just a few minutes.

EscapeArtist	Gateway
escapeartist.com	

Immediately bookmark this site – it could be your lifeline to living, working, and investing abroad. If you visit only one international website, make sure it's the unique EscapeArtist. It may at first overwhelm you with its massive amount of information and linkages. If you are a user of CEOExpress.com, you'll feel a kinship with this equally linkage-rich site. Operated by an expat living in the Caribbean, this is easily the Internet's most comprehensive website on everything from overseas jobs to investing, buying real estate, and living abroad. Even travelers find this site useful with its connections to ATMs, embassies, weather, visa requirements, cybercafes, world newspapers, and CIA World Fact Book. EscapeArtist usually tells it like it really is. For example, the site frankly states what it doesn't have on its site:

> We don't have a lot of nonsense about culture shock and 'how to keep in contact with home' chat-baloney. If you want to go, go; if you want to whimper, stay home. Home is where the heart's on fire.

From there it's all nuts-and-bolts on living and working abroad. This is the ultimate gateway international website with detailed country profiles, links to thousands of websites, online magazines, reference tools (maps, newspapers, search engines), message boards, videos, hundreds of articles, classified ads, and much more. Its overseas job section functions as a gateway site to international jobs:

escapeartist.com/jobs/overseas.htm

The site goes on and on. Indeed, you can literally spend days exploring this no-nonsense international site. Because this is such a large site and difficult to keep current with a limited staff, expect to find many URLs no longer working. If you use this site along with the search engine google.com, you should be able to cover most major international employment websites.

AIRS   **Gateway**
airsdirectory.com/jobboards

This is the ultimate gateway directory to over 3,800 job boards on the Internet – electronic classifieds, which include millions of job vacancies. Designed for employers who are interested in posting jobs, the site also is a rich resource for job seekers who are interested in identifying job boards relevant to their particular occupational areas. Most job boards include searchable job postings and many also allow job seekers to post their resumes online. The site includes hundreds of niche job boards that are often overlooked by job seekers. In addition to identifying 1,006 career hubs (general employment websites with job boards) in the United States, the site includes 329 international job boards, 898 industry job boards, 580 technical job boards, 192 healthcare job boards, and many others dealing with financial services (111), diversity (106), college and alumni (89), free agents (78), and newsgroups (190). The 329 international job boards are classified according to regions:

- International
- Africa
- Asia
- Canada
- Caribbean
- Central America
- Europe
- Middle East
- South America
- South Pacific

If, for example, you are interested in locating job vacancies in India, just click on to the Asia section where you will find 77 separate job boards; while several of these job boards cover numerous countries in Asia, including India, 21 job boards, as we go to press, specifically focus on jobs in India. The site also includes a search feature for locating job boards by name. You can easily spend hours playing around with this gateway site to the wonderful world of job boards. The international section allows users to search for job boards by region and country. While this is the most comprehensive gateway site for identifying job boards, it is by no means complete. The international section is at times spotty, overlooking many major regional and country job boards. Be sure to use search engines, such as google.com, in addition to this site to locate region- and country-specific employment sites.

The Riley Guide   **Gateway**
rileyguide.com/internat.html

Margaret Riley (now Margaret F. Dikel) is every job seekers' favorite online librarian – she knows where to find all the job and career "stuff," whether domestic or international. This is her site, a testimonial to what one very persistent and focused person can really do to create a useful gateway site to employment information and services on the Internet. While it is by no means complete, this site attempts to be comprehensive and succeeds to a certain extent. During the past eight years, Margaret Dikel has led a one-person crusade to compile one of the largest databases of career resources available anywhere. Organized around the key elements in a successful job search, the result has been "The Riley Guide" (rileyguide.com), a major gateway to career resources on the Internet – everything from career assessment, research, and networking to resume writing, cover letters, interviewing, and salary negotiations. Consisting of thousands of employment-relevant websites and articles organized by hundreds of useful categories, this site catalogs who is doing what on the Internet related to jobs and careers. It's not a fancy website with lots of functionality designed to stimulate one's desire for appealing colors, graphics, and interactivity. Instead, it's a bare bones site that delivers exactly what most job seekers need and want when they initially incorporate the Internet in their job search – lots of useful information and linkages about jobs and careers. Since the site is designed to "deliver the facts," you'll have to make your own judgments about the relative usefulness and value of the various sites and information that get catalogued in The Riley Guide. The international section includes numerous websites classified by regions and countries. Most of these websites are job boards. Many of the sites appearing on this website also are featured in Margaret F. Dikel's popular Internet job search book, *Guide to Internet Job Searching* (see order form at the end of this book or online at impactpublications.com).

Quintessential Careers	**Gateway**
quintcareers.com	

This is one of the richest gateway job search sites on the Internet. Unlike most employment websites, this one is designed for job seekers rather than employers and headhunters. As such, it focuses on each phase of the job search. The site includes numerous articles, a newsletter, and job search services. The linkages to other relevant sites are especially useful for job seekers in general and international job seekers in particular. Its "Quick Find" pull down menu takes users to a section called "Jobs – Geographic-Specific," which includes "Global & Worldwide Job Resources." This section includes international job sites as well as region- and country-specific sites. A good place to check on recommended sites as well as acquire lots of useful information on how to conduct an effective job search.

International Job Links	**Gateway**
www.joblinks.f2Scom/index_eng.htm	

This is a useful gateway site designed to assist both job seekers and employers in locating relevant international employment sites. It starts with a world map from which users can select particular regions for identifying job boards, job agents, recruiters, headhunters, and related sites. Sites are classified as to whether or not they offer job postings and resume databases.

About.com   **Gateway**
jobsearch.about.com/cs/internationaljobs1

This is the international employment directory section within the larger About.com site. It includes many useful resources to help individuals conduct an effective international job search. It covers such topics as international jobs, country information, etiquette abroad, international internships, international interviewing skills, international volunteer opportunities, online work abroad resources, international salary information, seniors living and working abroad, travel resources for global workers.

Going Global   **Gateway**
www.goinglobal.com

Launched in December 2001, this relatively new site is operated by Mary Anne Thompson, author of the popular *The Global Resume and CV Guide* (see the order form at the end of this book as well as impactpublications.com). The site extends the baseline work she did in the book on individual country employment profiles. Users can preview more than 25 country guides online – each of which run 50 to 75 pages when printed out – as well as purchase them in the form of e-books for $14.95 each. Individual country profiles examine key employment issues as well as cover work permits, visa regulations, key employers, employment websites, local recruitment firms, and more. The site also includes tips on writing resumes and CVs, links to career professionals in each country (local advisor teams of career management professionals), a newsletter, hot topics, and a global forum (message board). Primarily focusing on offering international job information, advice, consultation, and contacts on specific countries, the site does not include a job board nor a resume database. You'll need to click on to partner sites in order to access such functions. Plan to use this site for organizing a job search targeted on specific countries.

Students and others interested in finding short-term employment abroad, opportunities for teaching English abroad, or starting an international career should check out these four websites. They function as key gateway work, study, and travel abroad resources:

**University of Michigan   Gateway
International Center
umich.edu/~icenter/overseas/work/index.html**

Regularly updated by international resource guru Bill Nolting, who is the Director of the International Center, this is one of the most authoritative resources for keeping abreast of international resources relating to work abroad. It covers everything someone just starting out will find useful – international internships, short-term paid work opportunities, volunteering abroad, and teaching abroad (with or without certification). It also includes opportunities for students interested in government, engineering, science, law, and social work. Special sections offer information on working abroad in Spanish-, German-, and French-speaking countries as well as tips for minorities and women. You'll also find job search advice, linkages to work abroad programs, and linkages to its study and travel abroad programs and resources. If you want to know who is doing what and where, be sure to visit this rich site, which will quickly get you up and running with the right international resources.

**Transitions Abroad   Gateway
transitionsabroad.com**

This is the website of the publisher of *Transitions Abroad*, the most authoritative magazine on alternative study, travel, and work abroad. The site includes an excellent collection of international resources for students, graduates, experienced professionals, and seniors. It offers a comprehensive list of programs with ESL, special interest vacations, student overseas programs language schools, teen study and travel, senior travel, disability travel, volunteering abroad, internships abroad, and responsible adventure travel. It includes another section with online work, study, and travel abroad resources. If you're not sure if you want to travel, study, or work aboard – or do all three – be sure to survey the rich collection of resources available on this site.

iAgora.com	Gateway
iagora.com	

This is one of the most dedicated and enthusiastic groups of international-oriented students and professionals. It's literally an international community of individuals all over the world who are interested in work and study abroad. It's a great place to access resources as well as network with individuals in other countries. It includes separate sections on work abroad (entry-level and internships), study abroad, international travel, and networking groups (Forums, iClubs, iNotes, and chat). It also includes a classified section with ads from over 1,000 cities in 197 countries. Young people with a passion for international work and study will find this innovative site especially useful. Indeed, it's one of the few sites that allows individuals to engage in international networking.

JobWeb	Gateway
www.jobweb.com/catapult/interntl.htm	

This section of JobWeb's site for college students includes numerous resources for international students in the U.S. and for U.S. students going abroad. It also includes a searchable database of employers who hire college graduates.

Mega Employment Sites

Most international employment websites follow the standard job board format – lots of job postings and a resume database. Many of them also include information and advice on how to find an international job. While many websites only focus on international jobs or on specific countries, several large U.S.-based employment sites, such as Monster.com, Headhunter.net, HotJobs.com, and BrassRing.com, have developed international sections within their sites. This allows international employers to tap into their huge resume databases and large number of visitors that use these sites each day. However, as you will quickly see, only one such site stands out as an international employment leader – Monster.com. All the other mega employment websites, which are trying to develop international sections, pale in comparison to the depth and power of Monster.com's international profile. Nonetheless, many of the U.S.-based mega employment sites continue to expand their international scope as they attempt to be global employment sites rather than just American employment sites.

Monster Work Abroad   **Mega Site**
international.monster.com

Monster.com has a well deserved reputation for developing comprehensive and resource-rich specialty sites within its huge employment website. They've done it again in the case of this international employment sub-site. Integrated into the largest online employment site in the world – Monster.com – this international jobs section includes job postings, a resume database, a resume builder and manager, job search resources, career chats, message boards, articles, newsletters, relocation services, and more. Using the Global Gateway function (global gateway.monster.com), you can locate specific types of jobs in several countries around the world as well as acquire useful information on the particular country, including visas, housing, standard of living, education, transportation, attractions, currency, entertainment and more. The site's message board is especially active with dozens of questions asked and answered about various aspects of international jobs:

forums.monster.com/forum.asp?forum=119

You are well advised to browse through this section for information on working abroad. The site also includes numerous articles on working abroad, including information on teaching, interviewing, writing resumes, short-term work abroad, specific industries and professions, culture shock, relocation, visas, work permits, global etiquette, and international faux pas, city guides, and a bookstore:

international.monster.com/workabroad/articles

The only problem with this site is that it is easy to get lost in such a large and complex database. If you follow the URLs we've outlined for this site, you should be able to access a very rich database of information and advice. Individuals who are interested in immigrating to the United States should check out another related international message board entitled "Moving to the U.S. to Work," which is usually full of questions and answers regarding U.S. immigration laws and visa requirements, especially how to get a green card, OPT, and the H1B:

forums.globalgateway.monster.com/forumasp?forum=120

Monster.com also operates a global network of 19 country-specific sites. We identify the URLs for these sites at the beginning of Chapter 6.

Headhunter   **Mega Site**
headhunter.net

This is one of the largest employment websites with over 250,000 job postings and thousands of resumes in its searchable database. Recently acquired by careerbuilder.com, this site continues to operate as a separate employment website. It includes a special "International Job Search" section for jobs in Asia, Canada, India, and the United Kingdom. Its "International Select" section allows job seekers to search for over 35 types of jobs in all countries around the world. The search can be narrowed by keywords, educational background, and freshness of posting. However, while the site seems to have good functionality, not many international jobs appear to be in the database at the time of writing.

HotJobs	Mega Site
hotjobs.com	

This is another one of the largest employment websites on the Internet. In the process of being acquired by Yahoo.com at the beginning of 2002, HotJobs.com allows users to search its database for international job postings. However, doing so at present does not result in finding many jobs listed. HotJobs does have international sites in Canada and Australia. The Canadian site can be found at hotjobs.ca. The Australian site is actually a partner site which is powered by HotJobs: careerone.com.au. Searching for jobs in other countries through the HotJobs.com international location search engine results in few job listings. This situation may change in the future as HotJobs.com takes on a more international orientation.

FlipDog	Mega Site
flipdog.com	

This is one of the most popular and user-friendly employment websites with more than 500,000 jobs in its database. It literally crawls the web as it extracts job postings from employer websites. Always ranking in the top 10, it includes a special section on jobs outside the United States. This section includes a series of pull-down menus for selecting a country and then aligning it with particular job categories and employers. The database includes nearly 70,000 jobs outside the United States.

BrassRing   Mega Site
brassring.com

Primarily focused on technology and information, this site includes searchable job postings, a resume database, and a career center. International job seekers will especially want to connect to BrassRing's five international sites which are linked to this main site: Austria, Belgium, Canada, Germany, and the Netherlands. BrassRing is especially noted for sponsoring major career events, such as job fairs and hiring conferences. Be sure to check out their calendar of upcoming career events.

CareerJournal   Mega Site
careerjournal.com

Operated by the *Wall Street Journal*, this employment website primarily appeals to executives, managers, and professionals. It includes a lot of useful job search articles produced by *Wall Street Journal* writers and staff writers as well as salary information and job hunting advice. However, many sections of the site are actually operated by other companies through a network of affiliate relationships or partnerships. It includes related sites on jobs and careers in Europe and Asia. Its CareerJournalEurope is actually an affiliate relationship with eFinancialCareers:

www.efinancialnews.com/jobs

Its CareerJournalAsia section is an affiliate relationship with *The Asian Wall Street Journal, Far East Economic Review*, and futurestep.com, a site operated jointly by the executive recruitment firm of Korn/Ferry International and the Wall Street Journal. CareerJournal recently developed an affiliate relationship with www.goinglobal.com, which includes employment profiles on several countries (see above, page 53). Overall, there is little original international content on this site, and the number of international job postings is very small. You may want to periodically check this site for more international content.

Global and Multinational Sites

Several websites primarily specialize in international jobs. Global and multinational in orientation, most of these sites include searchable job postings and resume databases that cover numerous countries. Some sites also include useful job search information and advice on specific regions, countries, and employers.

Each of these sites tends to have its own particular orientation. Some sites are geared more toward young people in search of short-term international opportunities, whereas others are more suitable for seasoned professionals pursuing international careers. You'll have to examine each of these sites to determine which ones are most appropriate for your international interests. Several of the following sites are well worth exploring for possibly incorporating them into an international job search:

OverseasJobs.com	Global
overseasjobs.com	

This site is designed for professionals, expatriates, and adventure seekers. The site is especially responsive to the needs of resort professionals, college students, and recent grads. Employers post jobs and job seekers can post their resumes to the resume database operated by the parent company, AboutJobs. com. The site includes useful resources, such as an FAQ section and links to its other international-related sites – SummerJobs. com, InternJobs.com, and ResortJobs.com. Job seekers also can subscribe to the AboutJobs.com mailing list which periodically sends emails on career news, job hunting tips, site announcements, and employment opportunities with top employers.

PlanetRecruit   Global
planetrecruit.com

This popular international employment website is based in the
United Kingdom. It includes over 100,000 searchable worldwide job postings in its database with the following 20 countries being its most popular employment arenas: Australia,
Austria, Belgium, Canada, Denmark, Finland, France, Germany
Greece, India, North Ireland, Republic of Ireland, Italy, Japan,
Luxembourg, Netherlands, New Zealand, Norway, Portugal,
Saudi Arabia, Spain, Sweden, Switzerland, United Kingdom,
and the United States. Job postings can be searched by
keywords, locations, contract period, age of listing, and job
category (channel). Job seekers also can upload their resumes
(or CVs) to the site's database, register to receive emailed job
alerts, and acquire online advice. The job channels include
administrative and clerical, engineering, financial, graduate, IT
and telecommunications, media and arts, news media, and sales
and marketing. It also operates separate sites for the United
Kingdom and the Republic of Ireland.

Global Career Center   Global
globalcareercenter.com

This impressive new site includes a wealth of information on
countries (through worldship.com), work permits, and immigration (through workpermit.com). Job seekers can search for
international jobs in the site's database as well as post their
resumes to the online resume database. Jobs can be searched by
job category/title, country, salary range, employer, and keywords. Being a relatively new site, the number of international
job postings, along with resumes in the database, appear to be
limited.

Job Pilot International   Global
jobsadverts.com

While this international employment website primarily covers 15 European countries, it also includes the Middle East, Thailand, Australia, the United States, and a few other countries. The site allows job seekers to browse job postings for each country, submit a resume/CV to country-specific JobPilot sites, and acquire job search resources and information on work permits and visas. It includes a "Career Journal" section with tips on writing CVs, interviewing, negotiating salary, and resigning.

TopJobs.net   Global
topjobs.net

This employment website specializes in management, professional, technical and graduate positions. It primarily covers most of the key European markets (Ireland, Sweden, Switzerland, Norway, and the United Kingdom) and maintains affiliate relations with sites in Spain, Poland, and Thailand. Job seekers can search job postings by job category, industry sector, geographical region, and date. Job seekers also can browse company profiles and receive job opportunities via email. Its WAP service allows individuals to access the TopJobs site at any time and place by using a WAP-enabled mobile phone. Country sites have their own URLs:

- United Kingdom   www.topjobs.co.th
- Ireland   www.topjobs.ie
- Norway   www.topjobs.no
- Sweden   www.topjobs.se
- Switzerland   www.topjobs.ch
- Spain   www.topjobs.es
- Poland   www.topjobs.pl

- Thailand   www.topjobs.co.th
- International   www.international.topjobs.net

JobsAbroad.com   Global
www.jobsabroad.com

This site should be of special interest to young people, students, and recent graduates who are interested in acquiring work experience abroad as volunteers, interns, teachers, or in other types of paid positions. Individuals can search for job postings by job type and country. The site also includes information on study abroad, language schools, and budget travel as well as links to its other international study and travel site, GoAbroad.com (www.goabroad.com).

JobsBazaar.com   Global
jobsbazaar.com

This site includes over 12,000 jobs available in the United States, Singapore, Australia, United Kingdom, Canada, and India. Job seekers can research over 1,800 companies, post their resume online, blast their resume to over 4,100 recruiters, browse job postings, subscribe to a newsletter, join chat groups and a discussion forum, and use several useful tools and resources for calculating salary, relocating, and more. The site also includes information on visas and immigration and trips on departing for abroad and returning home.

International Career
Employment Center   Global
internationaljobs.org

This is primarily an international job listing newspaper. Individuals can subscribe online to two versions. The *International Career Employment Weekly* includes over 500 job vacancies each week. If you're not ready to apply for a job but want to observe what's available, you should subscribe to the monthly job listing newspaper, *International Employment Hotline*. The site includes a free job listing section called "Hot Jobs This Week." Many of the positions listed are with nonprofits, NGOs, and consulting firms engaged in development and relief work. Subscription rates for individuals range from $26 for 6 issues (6 weeks) to $280 for 98 issues (2 years).

Expatica	Global
www.expatica.com/jobs	

Designed for expatriates in search of jobs in Belgium, France, Germany, and the Netherlands, this site includes a handy search engine for finding jobs by key words, job category, country, salary level, and date of listing. The site also includes job search advice and numerous interesting articles on various aspects of living, working, and job hunting abroad.

Expat Exchange	Global
www.expatexchange.com	

This is one of the most comprehensive websites designed to assist expats with every aspect of living and working abroad. It includes an international job and career section which has a pull-down search engine for specifying individual countries. A search results in a linkage to an employment website that should have job listings related to the particular country. While this site does not operate its own job postings and resume database, it's worth visiting simply because of the larger international context within which it represents jobs.

Other useful sites worth checking out include:

- **Asiaco**   jobs.asiaco.com
- **First Worldwide**   firstworldwide.com.eo

- Workfinders   workfinders.net
- JobFactory   jobfactory.com

Expatriate Networks Abroad

Many individuals working in the international arena have landed jobs or acquired useful information, advice, and referrals through connections with expatriates. The good news is that the Internet has become the expatriate's best friend. It enables them to develop virtual communities for sharing information and advice and keeping in contact with each other via email, online newsletters, and message boards.

Expatriates operate numerous websites around the world. While many of these sites are country-specific, others are nationality-specific. They are excellent groups from which to learn about local living and working conditions as well as acquire information on such important issues as relocation, schools, housing, taxes, health insurance, travel, and doing business abroad. These sites yield a great deal of useful information and may offer some good opportunities to network with local expatriates.

Some of the major expatriate sites of interest to individuals living and working abroad include:

- AAFSW Foreign Service
  Lifelines   aafsw.org
- American Citizens Abroad   aca.ch
- Association of Americans
  Resident Overseas   aaro-intl.org
- Australians Abroad   coolabah.com
- BackToMyRoots   backtomyroots.com
- British Expats   british-expats.com
- Canadian Foreign Service
  Community Association   fsca-acse.org
- Canadians Abroad   geocities.com/canadians_
                                     abroad
- Foreigner in America   foreignerinamerica.com
- French Expatriates   www.expatries-france.com
- FT Expat   expat.ft.com/expat
- Expat Exchange   www.expatexchange.com

- **Expat Expert**   expatexpert.com
- **Expat Focus**   expatfocus.com
- **Expat Forum**   expatforum.com
- **Expat Grapevine**   expatgrapevine.com
- **Expatica**   expatica.com
- **Expatriates.com**   expatriates.com
- **Expatworld.com**   expatworld.com
- **Federation of American**
  Women's Clubs Overseas   fawco.org
- **Going-There**   going-there.com
- **Living Abroad**   livingabroad.com
- **Network for Living Abroad** liveabroad.com
- **Outpost**   www.outpostexpat.nl
- **People Going Global**   peoplegoingglobal.com
- **Women Abroad**   www.womenabroad.com

You will also find dozens of region-, country-, and city-specific expatriate websites. For example,

- **Americans in Greece**   geocities.com/Athens/7243
- **Americans in Prague**   americansinprague.com
- **Asian Expats**   www.asiaxpat.com
- **Belgium Expats**   www.xpats.com
- **Expat Hong Kong**   expathongkong.com
- **Expat Shanghai**   www.expatsh.com
- **ExpatAccess (Europe)**   expataccess.com
- **Expats in Brazil**   www.expat.com.br
- **Expats in Brussels**   www.expatsinbrussels.com
- **Expats in China**   www.expatsinchina.com
- **Expats in Denmark**   foreignshelp.dk
- **Expats in Pusan**   pusanweb.com
- **Expats in Singapore**   expatsingapore.com
                                aasingapore.com
- **Expats in Sri Lanka**   www.lankika.com
- **Expats in Thailand**   thailandtips.com
                                ethailand.com
- **Expats in Turkey**   ykcguide.com
- **ExpatVillage (Argentina)** expatvillage.com

- Gringoes.com (Brazil)   gringoes.com
- Japan in Your Palm   japaninyourpalm.com
- Living in Indonesia   www.expat.or.id
- Passport2Manila   passport2manila.com
- Prague TV   prague.tv
- Spain Expat   spainexpat.com
- Virtual Netherlands   www.xpat.nl
- Virtual Vienna   virtualvienna.net

For a comprehensive listing of over 100 expatriate sites, visit the expatriate linkage sections on EscapeArtist.com:

escapeartist.com/expatriate/expatriate1.htm
escapeartist.com/expatriate/expatriate2.htm

workopolis.com
CANADA'S BIGGEST JOB SITE

Home   Search Jobs   FastTrack   My workopolis   Resource Centre   Recruiters   Help

Françai
Boss Panic Butto

TELUS   OptionOne   Bank of Montreal   aeralex automotive

FastTrack Your Career

- Arts & Media   - Insurance
- ECommerce   - Legal
- Education   - Marketing
- Energy   - Retail
- Engineering   - Sales
- Executive   - Science
- Finance   - Skilled Trades
- Healthcare   - Students
- Hospitality   - Technology
- HR

Quick Job Search
- Keyword Search
- By Location
- By Date
- Now Hiring!

Resources

Resource Centre
- Search for Articles
- Career Advisors
- News & Views
- Tip of the Week
- Researching an Industry
- Share Success Stories
- MBA Program Search
- Add the Resource Centre to your PDA (with AvantGo)

All of us at workopolis.com wish you a safe and enjoyable New Year. Thank you for making 2001 such a success for us – we posted more than 330,000 jobs from more than 18,500 different companies – WOW! To give our employees a well deserved break, we will be operating with reduced staff during Christmas week, so if you require assistance, please be patient and we will assist you. Happy Holidays!

MY WORKOPOLIS

Save: Resumes, Searches & Job List

- Register for free as a new member or log in to create and save up to 10 Resumés
- Create an email CareerAlert! When was the last time a job found you?
- Track job opportunities that interest you in your personal job list
- Build and save job searches for re-use

THE GLOBE AND MAIL

Flight Centre ranked best employer
Keith McArthur (Friday, December 28, 2001)
Flight Centre Ltd., an Australian travel company that shuns offices, receptionists and secretaries, has come out on top of

THE 50 BEST COMPANIES TO WORK FOR IN CANADA
R.O.B. Magazine's third annual ranking of Canada's top employers
If you think there is a simple recipe for becoming a top-ranked employer, you won't find it in this year's Best Companies survey. As in the previous two years, the Top 50 are a very diverse group, with headquarters from Victoria to Halifax, and in businesses that range from travel to banking to selling chocolates.

LOOKING FOR NEWS YOU CAN USE?
First, check out our quick reference archive of useful material on topics such as job search techniques, interviewing, resume writing, job stress, dealing with bad bosses and more. For even more info, the Workopolis Subject Guide has classified our collection of 5,000+ articles by subject to make it easier to find what you are looking for.

Home   PowerSearch   Job Board   Employers   Agencies   Advice Centre   Advertisers   Contact   Help

SpeedSearch
Keywords e.g. Nurse

Legal Centre
Let our lawyers solve your problems

Training Courses
Search our wide range of courses

Employers & Recruiters
CV matching service here

Post your CV
Then let us find you a job

Top 10 Job Boards

1ˢᵗ jobs.telegraph
2ⁿᵈ GoJobSite
3ʳᵈ Workthing
4ᵗʰ JobTrack Online
5ᵗʰ Planet Recruit
6ᵗʰ Gis-a-Job
7ᵗʰ City Jobs Banking and Financial
8ᵗʰ TotalJobs
9ᵗʰ GAAPweb Accounting and Finance
10ᵗʰ SecsintheCity

Welcome to jobs.co.uk

jobs.co.uk is the leading UK recruitment portal. With over 500 job boards and recruitment sites in the UK, looking for a job can be a time consuming process.

We take the hard work out of finding a job on the internet by bringing together all the top UK job sites into one central location.

Featured Recruiters

Job Security Survey

How do you think recent events have affected people's job security?

Are you interested to know what other people are doing to improve their job security?

jobs.co.uk have some interesting results.

Click here for the details

Featured Recruiters

For The Best IT Jobs In The South West

www.eujobsite.co.uk

Engineers!

Register today for the chance to win a Nokia 9210 Mobile phone!

China International Employment Net

Chinese   English

- Job Position
- Resume Center
- Online Experts Forum System

Welcome to the
China International Employment Net

About China
Living in China
Working in China

6

Regional and Country Websites

HILE THE UNITED STATES HAS TAKEN THE lead in developing career planning and job search methods, recruitment approaches, and online employment sites, several companies in other countries have also moved into the online recruitment business by sponsoring regional- and country-specific employment websites. Numerous websites in Canada, the United Kingdom, Ireland, South Africa, India, Hong Kong, Japan, and Australia, for example, offer a variety of online recruitment and job search services for employers and job seekers alike. Most of these sites function as job boards, similar to the top employment websites in the United States, such as <u>monster.com</u>, <u>hotjobs.com</u>, <u>careerbuilder.com</u>, and <u>headhunter.net</u>.

Structure and Services

The structure and services of most regional- and country-specific sites are very similar. They include two or three basic elements normally associated with online recruitment sites that function as centers for connecting employers with job seekers:

- job postings (online classifieds)
- resume database and/or email job alert
- job search advice

While the sites are primarily sponsored by employers through advertising and user fees, job seekers can use most of these sites free of charge. Individuals normally can search online job postings by job title or category, location, and salary range. Some sites allow job seekers to upload their resumes into the site's searchable database whereas other sites provide an email alert option that informs job seekers of new job postings that relate to their interest criteria. Many sites also include useful articles on the employment process, chat groups, message boards, newsletters, career experts, and a few other services.

Visit and Re-Visit the Global Monster

None of the regional- and country-specific employment websites approach the scope and sophistication of the huge, and now increasingly global, U.S.-based Monster.com. Indeed, many job seekers are well advised to work through Monster.com's global network of multilingual employment websites. This constantly growing network now includes 19 region- and country-specific sites boasting more than 1,000,000 job postings worldwide:

▪ **Australia**	monster.com.au
▪ **Belgium**	monster.be
▪ **Canada**	monster.ca
▪ **Denmark**	monster.de
▪ **France**	monster.fr
▪ **Germany**	monster.de
▪ **Hong Kong**	monster.com.hk
▪ **India**	monsterindia.com
▪ **Ireland**	monster.com.ie
▪ **Italy**	monsteritalia.it
▪ **Luxembourg**	monster.lu
▪ **Netherlands**	monsterboard.nl
▪ **New Zealand**	monster.co.nz
▪ **Scotland**	monsterscotland.co.uk

- **Singapore**   monster.com.sg
- **Spain**   monster.es
- **Switzerland**   monster.ch
- **United Kingdom**   monster.co.uk
- **United States**   monster.com

Given Monster.com's current growth rate and acquisition plans, it should continue to add a couple of new countries to its global network each year. Depending on your specific country interests, you are well advised to get your resume into Monster.com's global network and frequently revisit its many affiliate sites around the world. You can quickly access any of the sites by going to the front page of any Monster site and clicking on to the various country flags that represent the affiliate site. Also, be sure to visit the rich international resource base we outlined on the U.S.-based Monster.com site in Chapter 5, especially the message board and resources sections which should help you realistically prepare for the global job market increasingly represented by Monster.com:

forums.monster.com/forum.asp?forum=119
international.monster.com/workabroad/articles

Canada

Canadians have developed numerous employment websites that provide quick access to job vacancies throughout their country. Many of these sites are city- and province-specific whereas others are nationwide. If you are Canadian or an expat wishing to work in Canada, be sure to explore the many websites that represent current employment opportunities in Canada. At the same time, you may want to review several of the U.S.-based employment websites outlined in Chapter 5. Many of these sites operate as "North American" websites and thus include Canadian job postings.

The sites identified in this section are primarily operated by Canadian government agencies and private organizations that understand the community-based nuances of the Canadian job market. Most of these sites are bilingual, offering both English and French language browsing options.

Major Canadian Sites

Sparsely populated and geographically expansive, Canada is one of the world's most highly wired countries with employment websites. Most Canadian sites include job postings and resume databases. Some sites also include useful career information and advice. Governments at all levels in Canada are very much involved in providing online employment information to the public. At the same time, several private companies have organized employment websites similar to the many job sites operating in the United States.

The following sites represent some of the largest and most comprehensive employment websites in Canada. They include a great deal of career information and services in addition to the standard job postings and resume databases.

Workopolis.com   **Mega Employment Site**
workopolis.com

This is one of Canada's largest and most comprehensive employment websites, which is affiliated with two major newspapers – *The Toronto Star* and *The Globe and Mail*. Well designed with numerous useful features, the site includes searchable job postings (30,000+ by job category, title, industry, and location), a resume database, and numerous online job search resources. The resource section includes career news, searchable articles, weekly tips, career advisors, industry research, success stories, education programs, surveys, and linkages to WorkNet and workplace columnist Bob Rosner.

Monster Canada   **Mega Canadian Site**
monster.ca

This is one of Monster.com's 19 global employment websites. Similar to other Monster.com sites, this one includes a resume database and job postings (more than 25,000) as well as a rich career resource section. The site includes a resume center, career articles and tips, forums, a practice interview center, interactive quizzes, a career horoscope, employer research center, and linkages to over 1 million international jobs. The site also includes an automatic email function which sends job seekers the latest job announcements. Like other Monster.com sites, this one includes an online poll.

Canjobs.com	Mega Job Board
canjobs.com	

Calling itself the "Canadian Employment Search Network," this employment website primarily offers searchable job postings and a resume database. Includes a quick search function to identify job listings by career type, province, and keyword. Also includes a network of separate websites for seven different provinces.

Numerous other Canadian employment websites include job postings, resume databases, email alert features, and job search tips. The following sites are primarily U.S.-based sites with Canadian sections or components:

- **Careerbuilder.com**   careerbuilder.com
- **ContractJobHunter**   contractjobhunter.com
- **ExecuNet**   execunet.com
- **FlipDog Canada**   flipdog.com/js/cat.html?_ requestid=923759
- **Headhunter.net Canada**   headhunter.net/JobSeeker/ Jobs/jobfindica.asp
- **HotJobs Canada**   hotjobs.ca
- **JobSniper Canada**   jobsniper.com

The majority of Canadian employment websites are operated by Canadian companies or the Canadian government. The following list of websites represents some of the best we have found for employment purposes:

- + Jobs Canada — plusjobs.ca
- ActiJobs — actijob.com
  canadajob.com
- ActualJobs Canada — actualjobs.com
- All Canadian Jobs — allcanadianjobs.com
- Alumni-Network — alumni-network.com
- AtlanticCanadaCareers — atlanticcanadacareers.com
- AtlanticJobs — atlanticjobs.com
- BrainsTalent — brainstalent.com
- Campus WorkLink — campusworklink.com
- Canada Career Consortium — careerccc.org
- Canada Job Centre — canadajobcentre.com
- Canada Job Search — canadajobsearch.com
- Canada Jobs — ijive.com
- CanadaIT.com — canadait.com
- Canadajobs.com — canadajobs.com
- Canadian Jobs — www.canadianjobs.com
- Canadian Careers.com — canadiancareers.com
- Canadian Employment Weekly — mediacorp2.com
- Canadian Jobs Catalog — www.kenevacorp.mb.ca
- Canadian Oil Field Jobs — jobs-canada.ca
- Canadian Public Service Jobs — jobs.gc.ca
- Canadian Resume Centre — canres.com
- Careerclick.com — careerclick.com
- Career Owl — careerowl.com
- Careers.org — careers.org
- CareerSite.com — careersite.com
- Charity Careers — charitycareers.com
- CharityVillage — charityvillage.com
- Job Bank Canada — jobbank.gc.ca
- Job Shark — jobshark.ca
- Jobs, Workers, and Careers — jobsetc.ca
- Newspaper Classifieds — workplace.hrdc-drhc.gc.ca/wantad.htm
- NetJobs.com — netjobs.com
- SkillNet.ca — skillnet.ca
- Yahoo! Canada (Jobs) — ca.yahoo.com

Career Information and Advice

While most employment websites focus on using job postings and resume databases, a few other sites primarily dispense online career information and advice. The following websites provide important research tools for job seekers who need to research industries, occupations, jobs, employers, and recruiters:

- Canada WorkinfoNet   workinfonet.ca
- Career Bookmarks   careerbookmarks.tpl.toronto.
                               on.ca
- Career Development Manual   www.careerservices.uwater
                               loo.ca/manual-home.html
- Career/Lifeskills Resources career-lifeskills.com
- Catapult   www.jobweb.com/catapult/
                               home/canada.html
- Contact Point   contactpoint.ca
- Directory of Canadian
  Recruiters   directoryofrecruiters.com
- Job Futures 2000   jobfutures.ca
- WorkSearch   worksearch.gc.ca

Research Sites

Numerous websites provide invaluable information on jobs, industries, and employers in Canada. The following websites represent only a few of the many useful sites for conducting research on the Canadian job market:

- Advice for Investors   fin-info.com
- Canadian Corporate News: ccn.ar.wilink.com/cgi-bin/
  Annual Reports   start.pl
- Canadian Trade Index   ctidirectory.com
- Canadian Information
  Centre for International
  Credentials   cicic.ca
- CorporateInformation   corporateinformation.com/
                               cacorp.html

▪ Newspapers/Magazines	•www.newspapers.com •canada.com/news •onlinenewspapers.com/ canada.htm •newsdirectory.com/news/ press/na/ca
▪ Research Company Information: Gateway	www.library.ubc.ca/lam/ company_intro.html
▪ SEDAR: System for Electronic Document Analysis and Retrival	sedar.com
▪ Strategis: Business Information By Sector	strategis.ic.gc.ca/sc_indps/ engdoc/homepage.html
▪ Strategis: Canadian Company Capabilities	strategis.ic.gc.ca/cgi-bin/sc_ coinf/ccc/cccsrch?submit_ srchscreen=basic&lang= e&search_screen=cc
▪ Strategis: Guide to Canadian Industries	strategis.ic.gc.ca/sc_indps/ gci/engdoc/homepage.html

Regional, Provincial, and Local Websites

Most regions, provinces, territories, and major cities have their own employment websites. Some of these sites are part of the Canjobs.com network. Depending on your geographic interests, the following sites may prove useful:

Alberta

▪ Alberta Government Job Board	www.gov.ab.ca/pao/jobs
▪ AlbertaJobs	albertajobs.com

British Columbia

▪ BritishColumbiaJobs	britishcolumbiajobs.com
▪ British Columbia Government Jobs	postings.gov.bc.ca

- City of Vancouver Jobs — city.vancouver.bc.ca/human resources/jobs/jobspage.html

Manitoba

- Manitoba Civil Service — gov.mb.ca/csc/jobs
- ManitobaJobs.com — manitobajobs.com

New Brunswick

- Atlantic Canada — careerbeacon.com
- AtlanticJobs — atlanticjobs.com
- BrainsTalent — brainstalent.com
- NBJobNet — nbjobnet.gov.nb.ca

Newfoundland

- Atlantic Canada — careerbeacon.com
- AtlanticJobs — atlanticjobs.com
- BrainsTalent — brainstalent.com
- NewfoundlandCareers — newfoundlandcareers.com
- Newfoundland Government Jobs — www.gov.nf.ca/psc/employment.htm
- NewfoundlandJobs — jobs.nf.ca
- NewfoundlandJobsite — newfoundlandjobsite.com

Northwest Territories

- Northwest Territories Government Jobs — www.gov.nt.ca/utility/jobs

Nova Scotia

- Atlantic Canada — careerbeacon.com
- AtlanticJobs — atlanticjobs.com
- BrainsTalent — brainstalent.com
- Jobs in Nova Scotia — jobsinnovascotia.com
- NovaScotiaJobShop — novascotiajobshop.ca

Ontario

- Go Jobs Ottawa   gojobs.gov.on.ca
- JobSearch.ca   jobsearch.ca
- JobSpotting.com (Ottawa) jobspotting.com
- OntarioJobs.com   ontariojobs.com
- OttawaJob.com   ottawajob.com

Prince Edward Island

- Atlantic Canada   careerbeacon.com
- AtlanticJobs   atlanticjobs.com
- BrainsTalent   brainstalent.com
- Prince Edward Island
  Government Jobs www.gov.pe.ca/jobs

Quebec

- QuebecJobs   quebecjobs.com
- QuebecJobSite   quebecjobsite.com

Saskatchewan

- Saskatchewan
  Government Jobs www.gov.sk.ca/psc/jobs
- Saskjobs.com   saskjobs.com

The United Kingdom

Numerous international and UK-specific employment websites provide a wealth of job search information and services, from job postings and resume databases to employment research and job search advice. Many of these sites also incorporate Ireland and several cities on the Continent. Similar to finding jobs in the United States and Canada, you can use the Internet to quickly gain access to thousands of job listings throughout the United Kingdom, enter your resume or CV into numerous online databases, and apply for jobs online, and use several online job search resources for sharpening your job search.

Gateway Employment Sites

While most employment websites in the United Kingdom are primarily job posting and CV database sites, a few function as useful gateway sites to job boards and related employment websites. Be sure to initially include these gateway sites in your job search:

Jobs UK	Gateway Site
jobs.co.uk	

This is the UK's premier gateway site to online job boards. It includes a "Quick Search" section for finding job boards by 30 occupational fields and 12 regional locations. It also includes a useful career resources section with information on writing a CV, interviewing, finding job discussion boards, linking to industries, locating salary data, and much more. Features the top 10 job boards. A very useful site for navigating through more than 500 UK job boards.

Ciao	Gateway/Evaluation Site
uk.ciao.com	

This site offers consumer reviews of numerous websites. Click on to the "Education and Careers" section which will take you to a list of the eight top employment ("recruitment agencies") sites. Consumers evaluate each site in terms of its database and search facilities, navigation, validity of job postings, frequency of content update, and ease of registration.

Three other websites also function as gateways to the world of employment sites in the United Kingdom:

- **Redundancy Help**   redundancyhelp.co.uk
- **Good Shop Guide**   thegoodshopguide.com/jobs.html
- **AIRSdirectory**   airsdirectory.com/jobboards

Top Employment Sites

Similar to U.S. and Canadian employment websites, numerous public and private organizations in the United Kingdom provide online employment information and services. Several major U.S.-based employment websites, such as <u>careerbuilder.com</u>, <u>headhunter.net</u>, and <u>flipdog.com</u>, include sections on the United Kingdom.

Several of the largest and most popular employment websites in the United Kingdom include:

Total Jobs <u>**totaljobs.com**</u>	**Mega Employment Site**

This site includes over 40,000 searchable job postings organized by occupational category, location, and keywords. It also allows job seekers to enter their CV online, research companies, review salary information, and assess their career health (site generates a free 8-page report). Includes career news.

Workthing <u>**workthing.com**</u>	**Mega Employment Site**

This popular site includes thousands of searchable job postings covering numerous job sectors. Offers a wealth of job search advice on everything from writing a winning CV to attracting a headhunter and negotiating salary. Job seekers can enter their CVs online and have new job announcements emailed directly to them. One of the few employment sites to offer unique content for numerous job sectors.

Jobpilot <u>**jobpilot.co.uk**</u>	**Mega Employment Site**

This user-friendly site offers one of the largest and most comprehensive collections of information and services to job seekers. Includes nearly 100,000 job postings, CV database, company profiles, and a "Career Journal" that includes CV tips, interview tips, negotiation strategies, resignation tips, and salary surveys. Includes special career channels for international job seekers, HR professionals, students, and legal issues. Also includes career news and information for foreigners wishing to work in the UK – work permits, visas, employment contracts, holidays, salaries, working hours, and how to get started.

Monster UK	**Mega Employment Site**
monster.co.uk	

Similar to Monster sites found in 14 other countries, this site is huge and comprehensive. Includes more than 30,000 job postings in its searchable database. Job seekers can create an online CV and upload it to the site's CV database. They also can have new job postings automatically emailed to them. The site is rich with job search information and tips, such as how to write a CV and prepare for a job interview, which are included in a "Career Centre." Includes featured employers, communities, relocation tips, and links to Monster's network of separate country sites.

Gojobsite	**Mega Employment Site**
gojobsite.com	

This site is largely oriented to the UK and European job market with its nearly 300,000 advertised job openings each month. Covers France, Germany, Ireland, Italy, Spain, and the United Kingdom (jobsite.co.uk). Includes a searchable database of nearly 40,000 job postings for 35 industry sectors, career news, job search advice, and more. Job seekers can elect to have new postings automatically emailed to them.

Fish4Jobs   **Mega Employment Site**
fish4jobs.com

This well designed site allows job seekers to search more than 40,000 job postings by title and location. Individuals also can explore different career paths which include information on responsibilities and duties, salaries, breaking in, training and qualifications, industry organizations, trade publications, and job listings. Also includes job-finding advice, recruiter profiles, and company information.

Gis-a-Job!   **Mega Employment Site**
gisajob.com

This well designed and flashy site allows job seekers to search for thousands of job listings by sector, location, type, and keyword. Job seekers also can enter and update their CV online, research jobs and agencies, explore top employment websites, survey news, receive job postings by email, and explore job search resources, such as how to improve one's CV and prepare for an interview.

Milkround   **Mega Employment Site**
www.milkround.com

Designed for graduate recruitment, this site includes numerous online employment opportunities with leading UK recruiters, job search advice, and employment news. Individuals can create their own online profile, apply online for jobs, receive job posting announcements and news by email, and complete an online personality assessment (Milkround Personality Questionnaire). This website also includes a "Learning City" which is powered by Wide Learning.

Numerous other employment websites provide a wealth of job search information, advice, and services. As with the previously featured sites, most of the following websites are primarily job boards with thousands of job listings and CV databases. Some sites specialize in a few occupational specialties.

- +Jobs UK — uk.plusjobs.com
- 1st Class Jobs — 1stjob.co.uk
- 3sectorsjobs — 3sectorsjob.com
- AgencyCentral — agencycentral.co.uk
- BigBlueDog — bigbluedog.com
- Brookstreet — www.brookstreet.co.uk
- Businessfile — businessfile-online.com
- CareerGlobe — careerglobe.co.uk
- City Jobs (UK & Europe) — cityjobs.com
- Contractor UK — contractoruk.co.uk
- CV-Library — www.cv-library.co.uk
- CVPoster.com — cvposter.com
- Cyber-CV.com — www.cyber-cv.com
- Cyberia — cyberiacafe.net
- E-job — e-job.net
- Education-Jobs — www.education-jobs.co.uk
- Employment Service — employmentservice.gov.uk
- First Division Jobs — www.firstdivisionjobs.com
- First-DivisionPeople — www.first-divisionpeople.uk.com
- First4London Jobs — first4london.com/jobs
- FTCareerPoint — ftcareerpoint.ft.com/ftcareerpoint
- Goldensquare — goldensquare.com
- Gradunet — www.gradunet.co.uk
- Guardian Unlimited — jobs.guardian.co.uk
- Homeworking.com — homeworking.com
- Qworx — qworx.com
- IT Job Bank — it-jobbank.co.uk
- Job Channel — job-channel.com
- Job Island — uk.jobisland.com
- JobMagic.net — jobmagic.net

- Jobs-At   www.jobs-at.co.uk
- Jobserve   www.jobserve.co.uk
- Job Shark   www.jobshark.co.uk
- JobSniper UK   jobsniper.com
- JobTrack   jobtrack.co.uk
- Jobzone   jobzoneuk.co.uk
- London Careers   londoncareers.net
- London Jobs Guide   www.londonjobsguide.co.uk
- Manpower   www.manpoweronline.net
- NetJobs   www.netjobs.co.uk
- New Monday   newmonday.com
- PeopleBank   peoplebank.com
- Personnel Store   personnelstore.com
- PhDjobs   phdjobs.com
- PlanetRecruit   planetrecruit.com/channel/uk
- Prospects   prospects.ac.uk
- Public Sector Jobs   jobs4publicsector.com
- QuantumJobs   www.quantumjobs.com
- Recruit-Online   www.recruit-online.co.uk
- Reed   www.reed.co.uk
- Secretaries   secsinthecity.com
- Stepstone   stepstone.co.uk
- TechJobs.co.uk   www.techjobs.co.uk
- Topjobs   topjobs.co.uk
- Total Jobs   totaljobs.com
- Travel Industry Jobs   www.travelindustryjobs.co.uk
- UK Contract Search   contract-search.com
- UK Jobs   ukjobs.com
- WorkTrain   worktrain.gov.uk
- Yahoo!   uk.yahoo.com

Career Information and Advice

A few employment-related sites primarily dispense job information and advice. The following sites are well worth visiting for tips on how to conduct an effective job search. They include numerous articles and expert advice on a wide range of employment subjects:

- Alec's Free CV, Job Hunting
  and Interview Tips   alec.co.uk
- Catapult   www.jobweb.com/catapult/
                                  home/uk.html
- Drjob.co.uk   drjob.co.uk
- Insidecareers   www.insidecareers.co.uk
- LineOne   www.lineone.net/business/
                                  jobs
- Pathfinder-One   www.pathfinder-one.com

Research Sites

Conducting research on companies, employers, and communities is essential to any job search. Consider including many of these websites in your research plan:

- 192 Enquiries   192enquiries.com
- Bird-online   bird-online.co.uk
- British Companies   www.britishcompanies.co.uk
- Business Guide   guide-u.co.uk/business
- Carol Annual Reports   carol.co.uk
- CorporateInformation   corporateinformation.com/
                                 ukcorp.html
- Corporate Reports   www.corpreports.co.uk
- Hoover's UK   hoovers.com/uk
- London Stock Exchange   londonstockexchange.com
- NewsNow   newsnow.co.uk
- Newspapers/Magazines   •onlinenewspapers.com/
                                  england.htm
                                 •newsdirectory.com
                                 •www.newspapers.com
- NISS (National Information
  Services and Systems)   www.niss.ac.uk
- Occupational Information   www.prospects.csu.ac.uk/
                                 student/cidd/occupat.htm
- The Times   www.thetimes.co.uk

JOBNET

- Job Search
- Job Browse
- Agency Directory
- JobSeeker's Toolbox
- News & Training
- Job Stats
- About JobNet
- Home

640x480 version

 WELCOME TO J⬤BNET
The Career Centre
for I.T. Professionals

JOBNET is the largest IT job search web site in Australia - with thousands of permanent, contract and consulting positions available for IT Professionals. The site also offers advanced features like a Daily Email Alert, Resume Storage and Announce your availability.

JOBSTATS is JOBNET's new industry indicator for the demand and supply of skills and services, check out what is hot in the market today!

JOBNET is in constant contact with recruitment agencies to ensure that job vacancies on this site are current. All jobs on JOBNET have been confirmed

the Career Centre for I.T. professionals

Watch out for the NEW JOBNET site next year!

jobpilot
.co.uk

Home For Employers PR/IR About us Contact us Help

jobpilot: Europe's career market on the internet

My jobpilot

Go to Jobs

Submit your CV

Career Journal

Job search

Never miss the job of your life

Select from 72425 vacancies worldwide*.

Job search   Submit your CV   New User

New to the game? Using online recruitment to get your next job

Time to move on Is making a change right for your career?

Career Journal Your resource for expert career advice.

Companies

Company services to match your recruitment needs

Services
+ Workflow
+ Job posting
+ CV database
+ Advertising

audited by
WWW

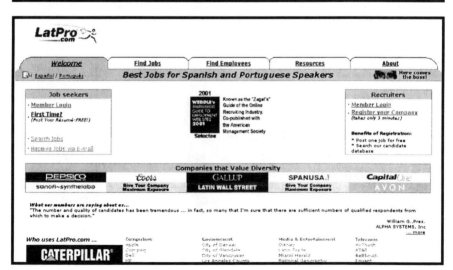

LatPro.com

Welcome | Find Jobs | Find Employees | Resources | About

Español / Português   *Best Jobs for Spanish and Portuguese Speakers*   Here comes the boss!

Job seekers
· Member Login
· **First Time?**
(Post Your Résumé-FREE!)
· Search Jobs
· Receive Jobs via E-mail

2001
WEDDLE's GUIDE TO EMPLOYMENT WEB SITES 2001
Selectee

Known as the "Zagat's" Guide of the Online Recruiting Industry. Co-published with the American Management Society

Recruiters
· Member Login
· Register your Company
(takes only 3 minutes)

Benefits of Registration:
* Post one job for free
* Search our candidate database

Companies that Value Diversity

PEPSICO   Coors   GALLUP   SPANUSA   CapitalOne
sanofi~synthelabo   Give Your Company Maximum Exposure   LATIN WALL STREET   Give Your Company Maximum Exposure   AVON

What our members are saying about us...
"The number and quality of candidates has been tremendous ... in fact, so many that I'm sure that there are sufficient numbers of qualified respondents from which to make a decision."

William G., Pres.
ALPHA SYSTEMS, Inc
... more

Who uses LatPro.com ...

CATERPILLAR

Computers
Apple
Compaq
Dell
HP

Government
City of Denver
City of Glendale
City of Vancouver
Los Angeles County

Media & Entertainment
Disney
Latin Trade
Miami Herald
National Geographic

Telecoms
AirTouch
AT&T
BellSouth
Sprint

In addition to Canada and the United Kingdom, many other regions and countries of the world have specialized websites that focus on jobs and employment. Many of these sites are rich with job listings as well as include resume databases to which you can post your resume. If you are interested in working in a particular region or country, you should check out several of these websites.

Africa

You'll find few online employment services for Africa as a whole or on specific countries within Africa. Not surprisingly, the largest number of employment websites focus on Africa's most developed and urbanized country – South Africa. Since many African countries are small and poor and thus cannot support independent employment websites, your best approach to individual countries is to refer to the major regional employment websites, such as findajobinafrica.com. Many job opportunities in Africa can be found with nonprofit organizations or NGOs, which we outline in Chapter 8 and which are partly listed on jobsearch.about.com/cs/ngosinafrica.

The Region

- **AfricaJobs** www.africajobs.net
- **Find a Job in Africa** findajobinafrica.com
- **Afriquemploi** afriquemploi.com
- **Jobs in Africa** jobsearch.about.com/cs/jobsinafrica
- **iciJob.com** icijob.com
- **Mbendi.co.za** mbendi.co.za/a_sndmsg/employ_menu.asp
- **Joblink** www.joblinkinternational.com
- **Asiaco Africa** jobs.asiaco.com/africa
- **WildNet Africa** jobspot.wildnetafrica.com
- **CareerMidEast.com** careermideast.com
- **Africa Online** africaonline.com
- **Africa Centre** africacentre.org
- **New Africa** newafrica.com

- Escape Artist   jobs.escapeartist.com/Openings/
                                 By_Location

Algeria

- 123Arab.com   jobs.123arab.com/Algeria_Job.
                                 html

Botswana

- Jobs in Botswana   www.botsnet.bw/jobs

Egypt

- Jobs in Egypt   www.jobsegypt.com
- Egypt Jobs   www.4arabia.com/eCareer/
                                 Jobs_In_Egypt
- EgyptNile   www.egyptnile.com/jobs
- Career Egypt   careeregypt.com
- Egypt Today   www.egypttoday.com
- 123Arab.com   jobs.123arab.com/Egypt_Job.
                                 html

Kenya

- Go Jobs Go   www.gojobsgo.com
- Kenya Job Site   www.kenyajobsite.com

Libya

- 123Arab.com   jobs.123arab.com/Libya_Job.
                                 html

Morocco

- Career Morocco   careermorocco.com
- Jobs Maroc   www.jobmaroc.co.ma
- Morocco Job Site   www.moroccojobsite.com

- 123Arab.com   jobs.123arab.com/Morocco_Job.
                                  html

Nigeria

- Nigeria Job Market   www.lagos-online.com/jobs_
                                  in_nigeria.htm
- Nigeria Job Site   www.nigeriajobsite.com

Rwanda

- Jobs in Rwanda   www.rawanda.net/english/JOB/
                                  JOBOPP.htm

South Africa

- Career Junction   careerjunction.co.za
- JobNavigator   www.jobs.co.za
- P-Net   pnet.co.za
- Jobs in South Africa   www.southafrica.co.za/
                                  busfin/employment.html
- EmployNet   www.employnet.co.za
- Job Food   www.jobfood.com
- South Africa Job Site   www.southafricajobsite.com
- WorkingForce Personnel   www.workingforce.co.za
- iafrica.com   careers.iafrica.com/topjobs
- Jobs-At South Africa   www.jobs-at.za.com
- Premier Personnel   www.premier.co.za
- Jobs in Port Elizabeth   www.pelinks.co.za/submain.
                                  asp?id=3095
- Work@za   www.mg.co.za.mg/work
- Jobline International   www.jobline.net/sa1.htm
- Cvonline   www.cvonline.co.za

Tanzania

- Jobs in Tanzania   www.ded-tanzania.de

Tunisia

- Career Tunis   careertunis.com
- 123Arab.com   jobs.123arab.com/Tunisia_
                              Job.html

Zambia

- Jobs in Zambia   www.zambiajobs.com

Asia

While many international job seekers are primarily interested in finding employment in their favorite European destinations, especially Italy, France, Spain, and the United Kingdom, the truth is that it's very difficult for anyone from a non-European Union (EU) country to secure employment in their countries, which often have high unemployment and very restrictive visa and immigration laws. Asia, on the other hand, is much more receptive to international job seekers. And those who have worked in Asia tend to find the international work experience there to be extremely rewarding. Indeed, many people who discover the joys of working in Asia much prefer it to Europe.

Asia boasts the world's largest labor force, with rapidly developing economies requiring increasingly talented workers. Consequently, many companies in Asia have developed employment websites for the region as well as for individual countries. In response to this unique labor market, Monster.com alone has developed separate employment websites for Hong Kong, India, and Singapore, major centers for Asia's growing high-tech job market. The Philippines and India continue to produce the largest number of high-tech and Internet specialists to which companies in the United States and other developed countries turn for labor sources.

While the economies of Asia have gone through difficult times due to the post-1997 economic downturn and subsequent recession, their labor markets remain relatively open to entrepreneurial international job seekers.

But one of the most interesting and promising international employment stories, and one of the best kept secrets among many job seekers in Asia, deals with teaching English. Indeed, many young people, as students or recent graduates, have quickly found their first international job by focusing on teaching English in Asia. As many of them will testify, one of the fastest ways to break into the international job market is through teaching in Asia. It has long been a good value region for backpackers, budget travelers, and adventuresome job seekers who found rewarding jobs teaching English in South Korea, Japan, Taiwan, China, and Thailand. Today more and more individuals with backgrounds in business, finance, communications, and information technology find employment in Hong Kong, China, Vietnam, Singapore, and India.

The following websites are well worth exploring when planning a job search targeted on Asia. Some of the best Asian sites, such as <u>asia dragons.com</u>, <u>asia-net.com</u>, <u>jobasia.com</u>, and <u>jobsdb.com</u>, are regional in nature, covering numerous countries in East, Southeast, and South Asia. Since teaching English remains one of the most popular international jobs in Asia, which requires few specialized skills or little experience, you also may want to include several of the teaching-English-abroad websites identified in Chapter 12. Most of these sites function as job boards with numerous searchable job listings. Many of them also include online resume databases.

The Region

■ Asiadragons	<u>asiadragons.com</u>
■ Asia-Net, Inc.	<u>asia-net.com</u>
■ JobsDB.com	<u>www.jobsdb.com</u>
■ Asiaco Jobs Center	<u>jobs.asiaco.com</u>
■ JobAsia	<u>jobasia.com</u>
■ Job Pilot, Asia	<u>jobsasia.com</u>
■ AsiaOne Careers	<u>careers.asiaone.com</u>
■ JobStreet	<u>jobstreet.com</u>
■ Asia-Links	<u>asia-links.com/asia-jobs</u>
■ FarEastJobs	<u>www.fareastjobs.net</u>
■ Asia-Employment	<u>asia-employment.com</u>
■ SearchBeat	<u>jobs.searchbeat.com/</u> <u>asiajobs.htm</u>
■ Jobs.net	<u>jobs.net</u>

- Jobs in Asia   jobsearch.about.com/cs/
                                  jobsinasia2
- Dragon Surf   dragonsurf.com/CareerWise/
                                  index.cfm
- WorldRoom   www.worldroom.com
- Mega Jobs Asia   www.fareastjobs.com
- Executive Asia   www.executiveasia.com
- Job Access   jobaccess.com
- TKO International   tkointl.com
- Firstworldwide.com   firstworldwide.com/eo
- EscapeArtist   escapeartist.jobs/overseas1.htm

Bangladesh

- Bdjobs.com   bdjobs.com
- Jobsbd   jobsbd.com

China

- JobChina.net   jobchina.net
- Zhaopin   www.zhaopin.com
- Hire China   www.HireChina.com
- China Career   chinacareer.com
- China International
  Employment Network   chinajob.com
- DragonSurf   www.dragonsurf.com/
                                  CareerWise/index.cfm
- Asiaco Jobs Center   jobs.asiaco.com/china
- Teach-in-China   teach-in-china.com
- All Jobs in China   china.career-agent.net
- Job OK   www.jobok.com

Hong Kong

- Hong Kong Job   hkjobs.com
- Job OK   www.jobok.com
- Monster Hong Kong   monster.com.hk
- Gemini Personnel Ltd.   gemini.com.hk/main.htm

- JobsDB — www.jobsdb.com/HK
- Asiaco Jobs Center — asiaco.com/hongkong
- PandaCareer.com — pandacareer.com
- Myjob — myjob.com.hk
- South China Morning Post — classifiedpost.com/jshome/php

India

- Monster India — monsterindia.com
- Career India — careerindia.com
- Careers India — careersindia.com
- CiolJobs.com — cioljobs.com
- JobStreet India — in.jobstreet.com
- a1jobindia.com — a1jobindia.com
- All India Jobs — allindiajobs.com
- Alltimejobs.com — alltimejobs.com
- Asiaco Jobs Center — jobs.asiaco.com/india
- BharatCareers — bharatcareers.com
- Career1000.com — career1000.com
- CareerAge — careerage.com
- Ciol Jobs — cioljobs.com
- DeccanJobs.net — deccanjobs.net
- Deevajobs.com — deevajobs.com
- HindJobs.com — hindjobs.com
- Hotel Jobs India — www.hoteljobsindia.com
- Humanlinks.com — humanlinks.com
- Indian Parttimejobs — indianparttimejobs.com
- Indobase.com — indobase.com/resumes
- jmmjobs.com — jmmjobs.com
- JobsAhead — jobsahead.com
- Jobs Omega — jobsomega.com
- JobsDB — www.jobsdb.com/IN
- JobStreet.com — www.jobstreet.co.in
- MIT Classifieds — mitclassifieds.com/employment.html
- Naukri.com — naukri.com
- Naukri2000 — naukri2000.com
- Placement India — placementindia.com

- Software Jobs India   softwarejobsindia.com
- Times of India   timesjobsandcareers.com
- Udyog.com   udyog.com
- Web India   webindia.com/india/jobs.htm
- ZDNetIndia   zdnetindia.com

Indonesia

- JobsDB   www.jobsdb.com/ID
- Karir.com   karir.com
- Asiasco Jobs Center   jobs.asiaco.com/indonesia
- Catcha.com   idcatacha.com/classified
- Indobix.com   indobix.com.job/index.asp
- Trade Indonesia   tradeindonesia.com/jobs.htm

Japan

- Jobs in Japan   jobsinjapan.com
- GaijinPot.com   gaijinpot.com
- Tokyo Connections   tokyoconnections.com
- CareerCross Japan   careercross.com
- Job Dragon   www.jobdragon.com
- Job Seek Japan   jobseekjapan.com
- Headhunter Japan   headhunter.jp
- Finding Jobs in Japan   kyushu.com/jalt/resourcejobs.
                              html
- WorkinJapan.com   workinjapan.com
- Asiaco Jobs Center   jobs.asiaco.com/japan
- HiJobs.com   hijobs.com
- InterCareer Net Japan   intercareer.com/japan
- Ohayo Sensei   ohayosensei.com
- Japanese Jobs   japanesejobs.com
- All Jobs in Japan   japan.career-agent.net
- AEC Japan   aecjpn.com
- Englishexpert Japan   englishexpert.com/japan

Korea

- Career Mosaic Korea   careermosaickorea.com
- Korea Job Link   koreajoblink.com
- Asiaco Jobs Center   jobs.asiaco.com/southkorea
- JobsDB   www.jobsdb.com/KR
- Teach Korea   teachkorea.com
- ESL Korea   eslkorea.com
- South Korea Jobs   www.southkoreajobs.com

Malaysia

- Job Island Malaysia   my.jobisland.com
- Jobs Malaysia   jobsmalaysia.com
- Job Street Malaysia   jobstreet.com.my
- JobsDB   jobsdb.com.my
- Catcha.com   www1.catcha.com.my
- Job Pilot   jobpilot.com.my
- Malaysia Job Center   newmalaysia.com/job
- Jobpolitan   jobpolitan.com.my
- Malaysia Career City   malaysia.cc
- Y2K Malaysia   Y2k.gov.my/employment
- Jobs.net Malaysia   jobs.net/locations/my/malaysia html

Pakistan

- Ecareers   ecareers.com.pk
- Jobware Pakistan   pk.jobware.com
- Asiaco Jobs Center   jobs.asiaco.com/pakistan
- Pakistan Jobs   www.pakistanjobs.com

The Philippines

- Inq7.net   www.inquirer.net
- JobStreet Philippines   ph.jobstreet.com
- Asiaco Jobs Center   jobs.asiaco.com/philippines
- JobsDB   www.jobsdb.com/PH

- The Job Page   thejobpage.com
- Yehey   jobs.yehey.com

Singapore

- **Monster Singapore**   monster.com.sg
- **Singapore Jobs**   www.singapore-careers.com
- **9to5.com**   9to5.com.sg
- **CareerZone**   careerzone.com.sg
- **JobStreet Singapore**   sg.jobstreet.com
- **Asiaco Jobs Center**   jobs.asiaco.com/singapore
- **JobsDB**   www.jobsdb.com/sg
- **Catcha.com**   www1.catcha.com.sg
- **JobAsia**   jobasia.sg
- **JobmarketSingtao.com**   jobmarketsingtao.com
- **Jobmaster**   jobmaster.com.sg
- **Job Pilot**   jobpilot.com.sg
- **Jobsite**   www.jobsite.com.sg

Sri Lanka

- Sri Lanka Jobs   info.lk/jobs
- LankaWeb   lankaweb.com/classified/jobs.html
- Asiaco Sri Lanka   srilanka.asiaco.com

Taiwan

- DragonSurf   www.dragonsurf.com/CareerWise/index.cfm
- Asiaco Jobs Center   jobs.asiaco.com/taiwan
- JobsDB   www.jobsdb.com/tw
- Teach in Taiwan   teach-in-taiwan.com

Thailand

- Job Search Thailand   th.jobaa.com
- Jobs in Thailand   escati.com/thaijobs.htm

- Job Pilot   jobpilot.co.th
- JobTopGun   www.jobtopgun.com
- Asiaco Jobs Center   jobs.asiaco.com/thailand
- JobsDB   www.jobsdb.com/TH
- eThailand.com   ethailand.com
- Bangkok.Com   bangkok.com/jobs
- Top Jobs in Thailand   topjobs.co.th
- Teach in Thailand   teach-in-thailand.com

Vietnam

- Vietnam Online   vietnamonline.com/employex
- Jobs in Vietnam   www.intel.com/jobs/vietnam
- Asiaco Jobs Center   jobs.asiaco.com/vietnam
- Vietjob   vietjob.com
- Vietnam Jobsite   www.vietnamjobsite.com

Australia, New Zealand, and the Pacific

The South Pacific encompasses a diverse collection of tiny to large islands and the continent of Australia. Sparsely populated, a few countries in this region offer a variety of job opportunities for enterprising job seekers. Most of these opportunities are centered on Australia, New Zealand, and Guam.

Being "down under" and relatively isolated from major centers of the world, Australia has been very active in getting wired via the Internet. In addition, career planning and job search have become popular in Australia, following the patterns found in the United States, Canada, and the United Kingdom. As a result, you'll find numerous Australian employment websites providing job search information and services. While many of the sites are general, some sites specialize in particular occupations, such as information technology, nursing, sports, and hospitality industries. If you need information on Australian immigration laws and regulations, be sure to visit the official online source for this information:

hwmigration.com/?col_referral

The following website functions as a gateway directory to jobs in both Australia and New Zealand:

http://intljobs.about.com/careers/intljobs/cs/jobsinausnz/seindex.htm

Australia

- **Australia JobSearch**   jobsearch.gov.au
- **Employment Australia**   employment.com.au
- **SEEK**   seek.com.au
- **MyCareer Australia**   mycareer.com.au
- **JobNet**   jobnet.com.au
- **Monster Australia**   monster.com.au
- **Careers Online**   careersonline.com.au
- **JobsPlus**   jobsplus.com.au
- **JobWeb**   jobweb.com.au
- **Byron Employment Australia**   employment.byron.com.au
- **Asiaco Jobs Center**   jobs.asiaco.com/australia
- **Careerone** (HotJobs)   careerone.com.au
- **Get a Job**   getajob.com.au
- **Jobz.com**   jobz.ozware.com
- **Positions Vacant**   positionsvacant.com.au
- **+Jobs Australia**   au.plus.jobs.com
- **IT Jobs MyCareer**   itjobs.mycareer.com.au
- **ZDNet Australia Tech Jobs** zdnet.com.au/jobs
- **Jobs in Australia**   jobs-australia.com
- **Jobnet.com** (IT)   jobnet.com.au
- **Australian IT**   australianit.news.com.au
- **Jobs Australia**   jobsaustralia.com.au
- **Hospitality Jobs**   hospitalityjobs.com.au
- **Cool Jobs Australia**   cooljobsaustralia.com
- **Jobs-At Australia**   www.jobs-at.au.com
- **Australia Employment Center**   asiadragons.com/australia/ employment
- **Superstaff**   superstaff.com.au
- **Youth Jobs Australia**   youthjobs.com.au
- **Nursing Jobs Australia**   nursingjobs.com.au

- Sport Employment   www.sportemployment australia.com.au
- Working in Australia   www.workingin.com/au/ IT & T   index/asp
- Australiajobs.com   australiajobs.com
- Go Career   gocareer.gov.au

New Zealand

- New Zealand Search   nzsearch.co.nz/category. (Employment)   asp?id=633
- Monster New Zealand   monster.co.nz
- Employment New Zealand   employment.co.nz
- New Zealand Jobs   www.nzjobs.co.nz
- JobUniverse   www.jobuniverse.co.nz
- All Jobs New Zealand   alljobs.co/nz/index.htm
- SEEK   seek.co.nz
- Jobstuff   jobstuff.co.nz
- New-Zealand-Jobs   new-zealand-jobs.com
- Working in New Zealand   www.workingin.com/nz/ index/asp

Guam

- Jobs on Guam   www.jobsonguam.com
- Guam's Job Bank   www.ajb.org/gu
- Job Factory   jobfactory.com/s/f_guam.htm

Europe

Finding a job in most European countries can be a daunting task for anyone from outside the EU community. Restrictive immigration laws coupled with preferences for hiring local labor mean landing a job in Europe is a real challenge. Several of the major employment websites, such as JobPilot.co.uk, include information about visas, work permits, and immigration laws. Nonetheless, if you offer unique skills, have the right contacts, and are persistent, you should be able to break into this difficult job market. But be sure to review the immigration restrictions outlined at <u>workpermit.com</u> for 11 European nations.

Several employment websites cover Europe as a whole, parts of Europe (three to seven countries), and individual countries. As we noted earlier in this chapter, the most highly wired country is the United Kingdom, which has dozens of websites focused on the recruitment and job search processes. Ireland also is highly wired with many specialty employment websites. Several sites in Belgium also cover other countries in Europe. Some countries, such as Turkey, Greece, Croatia, Bosnia-Herzegovina, Georgia, Ukraine, Belarus, Slovakia, Slovenia, Serbia/Montenegro, Macedonia, Moldova, Albania, and Portugal have yet to offer major employment-related websites. Some jobs in these countries may be represented on the regional sites.

Since we've already examined the United Kingdom, this section covers most other countries in Europe. Many of the individual country websites tend to specialize in recruiting computer and information technology specialists.

The Region

- EU-Jobs   www.EU-Jobs.net
- 1Job.net   1job.net
- Stepstone   www2.stepstone.com
- Jobs in Europe   topjobs.net
- DotJobs   www.dotjobs.co.uk
- Jobs in UK and Europe   www.datumeurope.com
- Jobs Europe   jobs-europe.com
- Eurojobs   eurojobs.ocm
- ActiJob.com   europejob.com
- Europe Jobs   europejobs.net
- EuroJobs   www.eurojobs.com
- JobPilot   jobpilot.co.uk
- Asiaco Jobs Center   jobs.asiaco.com/europe

Austria

- Austropersonal.com   austropersonal.com
- JobPilot Austria   jobpilot.at
- AMS IT   www.ams.or.at/itjobs

Belgium

- 1Job.net   1job.net
- Monster Belgium   monster.be
- Belgium-Jobs   belgium-jobs.net
- Jobat.be   www.jobat.be
- Ego-Search   www.egosearch.be
- Newmonday.com   www.newmonday.be
- Vacature.com   www.vacature.com
- Jobs Today   www.jobstoday.be
- Jobscareer.be   www.jobs.be
- JobUniverse   www.jobuniverse.be

Cyprus

- jobs.com.cy   jobs.com.cy

Czech Republic

- JobMaster   jobmaster.cz
- CV-Online Czech Rep.   cvonline.cz
- JobPilot Czech   jobpilot.cz

Denmark

- +Jobs Denmark   denmark.plusjobs.com
- Job-Index   jobindex.dk
- All Jobs in Denmark   denmark.career-agent.net

Estonia

- CV-Online Estonia   www.cv.ee

France

- Monster France   monster.fr
- JobPilot   jobpilot.fr

Germany

- Monster German   monster.ge
- Jobs-Germany   jobs-germany.de
- JobPilot   jobpilot.de
- Jobs   jobs.de
- Jobware   jobware.de
- ZDNet   zdnet.stepstone.de
- Yahoo Germany   de.join.yahoo.com

Hungary

- CV-Online Hungary   www.cvonline.hu

Ireland

- All Jobz.com   alljobz.com
- Monster Ireland   monster.com.ie
- Belfast Telegraph   www.belfasttelegraph.co.uk:
                          8008/jobfinder
- Irishjobs   www.irishjobs.ie
- Jobs-Ireland   jobs-ireland.com
- Jobs Ireland   www.jobsireland.com
- Recruit Ireland   recruitireland.com
- Netnation IT Recruitment   www.netnation.ie
- All Jobs in Ireland   jobs-in-ireland.com
- Job Track Ireland   jobtrack.ie
- Jobs Nation   www.jobsnation.net
- IT People   itpeople.ie
- Ireland Hiring   irelandhiring.com
- Stepstone   www.stepstone.ie
- Jobs.ie   jobs.ie
- JobZone   jobzone.ie
- NIJobs   nijobs.com
- Recruit NI   recruitni.com
- TopJobs   topjobs.ie
- Hotel Jobs   www.hoteljobs.ie
- Hotel Jobs Ireland   hoteljobsireland.com

Italy

- Monster Italy   monster.com.it
- JobOnline   www.jobonline.it
- All Jobs in Italy   italy.career-agent.net
- JobPilot   jobpilot.it

Latvia

- CV-Online Latvia   cv.lv

Lithuania

- CV-Online Lithuania   cvonline.lv

The Netherlands

- Monster Netherlands   monsterboard.nl
- Jobs   jobs.nl
- 1Job.net   1job.net/ned.htm
- Arbeidsmarkt.com   arbeidsmarkt.com
- EnglishLanguageJobs   www.englishlanguagejobs.com

Norway

- Topjobs   topjobs.no
- All Jobs in Norway   norway.career-agent.net

Poland

- Jobs   jobs.pl
- CV-Online Poland   cv.pl
- Topjobs   topjobs.pl
- JobPilot   jobpilot.pl

Portugal

- e-Jobs Portugal   www.e-jobs.pt

- CVlatino   cvlatino.com

Romania

- 1job.ro   1job.ro
- HumanResources.Ro   humanresources.ro
- JobSearch Romania   www.jobsearch.ro

Russia

- Moscow Times Career
  Center   www.careercenter.ru
- All Jobs in Russia   russia.career-agent.net
- Human Resources On-line   hro.ru
- St. Petersburg Times   sptimesrussia.com/727/jobs/
                                index.htm?734curr

Spain

- InfoJobs.net   infojobs.net
- TopJobs   topjobs.es
- JobPilot   jobpilot.es
- Monster Spain   monster.es
- CVlatino   cvlatino.com

Sweden

- Topjobs   topjobs.se

Switzerland

- Topjobs   topjobs.ch
- JobPilot   jobpilot.ch
- Math Jobs   math-jobs.ch

Central and South America

Employers in Central and South America are only beginning to use the Internet for recruitment purposes. Internet usage is not widespread within these regions. Unlike North America, Asia, or Europe, you'll only find a few regional and country employment sites for Central and South America, including the Caribbean.

The Region

- Laborum   www.laborum.com
- LatPro.com   latpro.com
- NetEmpleo   netempleo.com
- JobShark   jobshark.com
- South America Jobs   www.southamericajobs.net
- Trabajos   trabajos.com
- Asiaco Jobs Center   jobs.asiaco.com/latinamerica
- CVlatino   cvlatino.com
- Job Search   jobsearch.about.com/cs/
                                 latinamericajobs

Argentina

- EIStaff.com   elstaff.com
- Red de empleo   reddeempleo.com
- Weblaboral   www.weblaboral.com.ar

Brazil

- Catho Online   catho.com.br
- Curriculum   www4.curriculum.com.br
- Curriex   www.curriex.com.br

Mexico

- Mexico-Jobs   mexico-com.com/employers.
                                 htm
- All Jobs in Mexico   mexico-career-agent.net

- **MexPlaza**   clasificados.mexplaza.com.mx
- **BolsaTrabojo**   www.bolsa-trabojo.com
- **Empleoshoy**   www.empleoshoy.com

Middle East

Similar to Central and South America, the Middle East has very few employment websites. However, numerous international employment opportunities are available in several Middle East countries, especially Saudi Arabia and Israel. A few regional sites include a limited number of job postings.

The Region

- **4arabia**   www.4arabia.com/eCareer
- **Bayt**   web1.bayt.com
- **123 Arab**   jobs.123arab.com
- **Career Mideast**   careermideast.com
- **Asiaco Jobs Center**   jobs.asiaco.com/middleeast
- **Arabian Careers**   arabiancareers.com
- **Middle East Jobs**   http://intljobs.about.com/
                                  careers/intljobs/cs/middleeast
                                  jobs/index.htm

Iran

- **Iran Central Net**   iran-central.net/jobs.htm
- **Profil**   profil.si

Israel

- **Computer Jobs**   cji.co.il
- **Job Net**   jobnet.co.il

Saudi Arabia

- **The HAK Group**   saudijobs.com
- **Saudi Recruitment**   saudirec.com

- National Career
  Networking Association   ncna.com/saudi.html

Syria

- Syria Recruitment   syriarec.com

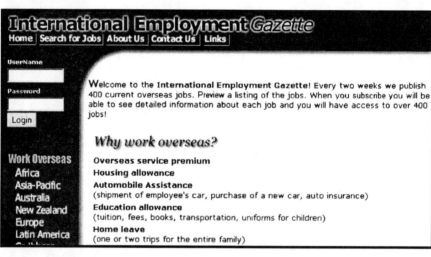
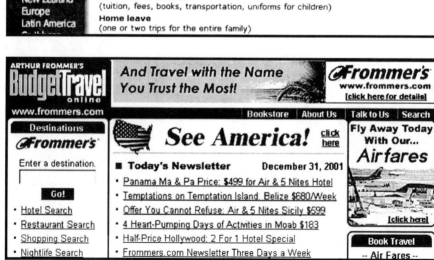

7

Employment and Travel Publishers

NUMEROUS PUBLISHERS SPECIALIZE IN PRODUCING international employment and travel materials. Primarily publishing books and newsletters, some offer job listings and advice on how to find an international job. Many publishers who produce destination travel guides maintain their own websites which provide online travel information (hotels, restaurants, transportation, sightseeing), reservation centers, specials, bookstores, and bulletin boards and community forums. These can be useful sites for researching specific destinations and arranging travel when living abroad.

Employment-Related Publishers

The publishers listed below specialize in producing information on how to find an international job. Operating like classified advertisers, the first two produce both online and offline international job listings, which are available to users for various monthly and yearly subscription fees. You can visit their websites for information on how to subscribe to their publications as well as browse sample listings. The final two publishers provide some useful online overseas employment information:

- **International Employment
  Gazette** (biweekly)   www.intemployment.com
- **International Career
  Employment Center** (weekly) internationaljobs.org
- **Overseas Jobs Express**   overseasjobs.com
- **Overseas Digest**   overseasdigest.com

Several book publishers specialize in producing and distributing a variety of books on finding international jobs and working abroad. They include such popular titles as *International Jobs Directory*, *Work Abroad*, *Live and Work in France*, and *Work Your Way Around the World*. Many of these resources are difficult to find in bookstores and libraries, but they can be ordered online from the publishers. Impact Publications pulls together most of these resources, including many popular culture shock, etiquette, and travel guidebooks, in their comprehensive international job catalog – *Work, Study, and Travel Abroad* – which can be downloaded from the front page of their website: impactpublications.com. The major such publishers include:

- **Impact Publications**   impactpublications.com
- **Transitions Abroad**   transitionsabroad.com
- **Vacation Work**   vacationwork.co.uk
- **Peterson's**   petersons.com
- **How to Books**   www.howtobooks.co.uk
- **Seven Hills Distributors**   sevenhillsbooks.com
- **Intercultural Press**   interculturalpress.com
- **Graphic Arts Center
  Publishing Company**
  (*The Culture Shock Series*)   gacpc.com
- **Canadian Guide to Working
  and Living Overseas**   workingoverseas.com
- **Uniworld Business
  Publications, Inc.**   uniworldbp.com
- **Living Abroad Publishing**   livingabroad.com
- **Living Overseas**   livingoverseas.com

Several other publishers, such as Wiley, Avalon, Ten Speed Press, Surrey, and Perseus Press, occasionally produce one or two books dealing with international jobs. You can easily find these publications by using the two major online bookstores as a books-in-print search engine: amazon.com and bn.com. The Barnes and Noble site (bn.com) tends to yield the best search results.

Travel Planning on the Internet

One of the great attractions of living and working abroad is travel. Indeed, many individuals who seek international jobs simply love to travel. Experiencing the best of both worlds is having a home country based job that also allows them to travel abroad.

International jobs inevitably involve some form of travel planning which involves visas, airline tickets, accommodations, language, insurance, shipping, culture, tipping practices, car rentals, sightseeing, entertainment, and specific destinations. The following books identify thousands of travel-relevant websites. Anyone planning to work or live abroad should consult these comprehensive directories. These publications will save you hours of time and effort in using search engines to sort through the jungle of travel websites:

- *Buying Travel Services on the Internet*
- *The Complete Idiot's Guide to Planning a Trip Online*
- *Michael Shapiro's Internet Travel Planner*
- *Practical Nomad Guide to the Online Travel Marketplace*
- *Online Travel*
- *Sam's Teach Yourself E-Travel Today*
- *Travel Planning on the Internet*
- *Travel Planning Online for Dummies*

Most of these books are available in bookstores and through Impact Publications (impactpublications.com).

Some of the best portals or gateway sites for doing travel planning on the Internet include the following:

- **Kasbah**   kasbah.com
- **Travel Library** travel-library.com

- VirtualTourist
- Travelnotes
- My Travel Guide
- Planetrider
- TravelPage
- Travel-Guide
- Travel.com
- Worldroom

virtualtourist.com
travelnotes.org
mytravelguide.com
planetrider.com
travelpage.com
travel-guide.com
travel.com
worldroom.com

Destination Publishers

The heart of travel publishing lies with several publishing companies that produce a series of general and niche travel guidebooks. Most of these companies maintain websites, which include some online information on various destinations but may also include a full range of travel information and services. As content providers, these publishers' websites offer a great deal of useful information on countries and communities. Browsing through the following websites will uncover hundreds of useful travel guidebooks:

- Frommer's
- Fodor's
- Lonely Planet
- Rough Guides
- Rick Steves
- Impact Publications

- Moon Handbooks
- Footprint

- Globe Pequot
- Columbus Publishing
- Let's Go
- Travelers' Tales
- Hunter Publishing
- Michelin
- Ginkgo Press
- Avalon Travel Publishing

frommers.com
fodors.com
lonelyplanet.com
roughguides.com
ricksteves.com
impactpublications.com
ishoparoundtheworld.com
moon.com
www.footprint-handbooks.
co.uk
www.globe-pequot.com
wtg-online.com
letsgo.com
travelerstales.com
www.hunterpublishing.com
www.michelin-travel.com
ginkgopress.com
travelmatters.com

If you are primarily interested in downloading travel e-books from the Internet, visit Publications Unbound, which includes hundreds of travel books in e-book form: publicationsunbound.com. The same e-books and others, including Going Global's country employment profiles, are available in the e-book section of impactpublications.com.

idealist.org

Action Without Borders

First time here? | About us | Help

Idealist en español

Click on the pictures above to visit some of the organizations you'll find here

[ ] [Organizations ▾] [Search]

For Organizations
Post job openings, events,
services, resources and
volunteer opportunities

FIND
in 153 countries:

Organizations (24,922)

Jobs (1,167)

Volunteer

My Idealist
Register for personal email
updates with new listings
matching your interests

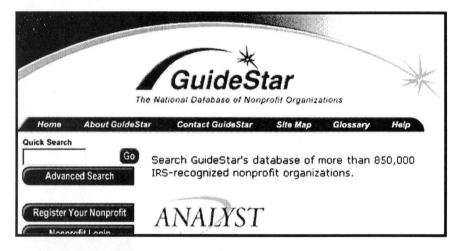

GuideStar

The National Database of Nonprofit Organizations

Home   About GuideStar   Contact GuideStar   Site Map   Glossary   Help

Quick Search

[ ] [Go]

Advanced Search

Search GuideStar's database of more than 850,000
IRS-recognized nonprofit organizations.

Register Your Nonprofit

Nonprofit Login

ANALYST

[JOIN NOW] [SEARCH [ ]] [GO]

INDEPENDENT SECTOR

member area   about us   issues   research   public policy   newsroom

A coalition of leading nonprofits, foundations, and corporations strengthening not-for-profit initiative, philanthropy, and citizen action.

President's
Corner

Giving and
Volunteering

Charity
Lobbying in
Public Interest

Member
Profiles

Publications

Annual
Conference

Events

Awards

Wired, Willing, and Ready: A
new survey by INDEPENDENT
SECTOR and Cisco Systems finds
technology boosts nonprofits'
effectiveness. Press Release

IS Member Briefing: On
December 6, Leslie Lenkowsky,
newly appointed CEO of the
Corporation for National and
Community Service, addressed IS
members about the evolution of
his organization and the future of
service in America. Transcript

ATLANTA
2001 Thank you for joining
us for IS's 2001

**INDEPENDENT SECTOR Survey
Measures the Everyday
Generosity of Americans**

■ **89%** of American families made
charitable contributions last year.
■ **44%** of adults volunteered their
time.

Read more key findings on
Americans' charitable behavior in
*Giving and Volunteering in the
United States 2001.*

**INDEPENDENT SECTOR Survey
Finds Mixed Outlook on
Charitable Giving. IS presents**

**NONPROFIT
PATHFINDER**
The global gateway to civil
society research and innovation.

GiveVoice.org
Speak out for change

IS Survey Measures
the Everyday Generosity
of Americans

8

Nonprofits and Educational Groups

ONPROFIT ORGANIZATIONS, WHICH ARE VARI-
ously called PVOs (private voluntary organizations) and
NGOs (non-governmental organizations), provide numerous international employment opportunities for individuals
interested in the nonprofit world. Consisting of more than 100,000
value-driven organizations, it's a world where purpose is more important than profit. Many of these nonprofits compete with private
contracting and consulting firms for government funding of programs
and projects. All are involved in some form of private and public fund-
raising to support their operations and causes.

Causes and Missions

You may be familiar with several of the nonprofit organizations
outlined in this chapter because of their high public profiles. Groups
such as the American Red Cross, Habitat for Humanity, National
Wildlife Federation, Population Council, Salvation Army, Save the
Children Federation, and The Sierra Club are very active in raising
funds as well as generating public awareness of their humanitarian and

environmental missions. Thousands of other less well-known nonprofit organizations are deeply involved in a variety of worthwhile causes worldwide: child survival, refugee and disaster relief, self-help income generation, enterprise development, vocational training, agriculture and food production, population planning, communications, social welfare, environment and natural resource management, housing, health care, and community development. Some of these organizations are quasi-religious and thus combine evangelical elements with their humanitarian missions – religious and secular operations, the separation of which is not always clear.

Many seasoned international workers initially broke into the international job market by working for a nonprofit organization as either a volunteer or paid staff member. In fact, this is still one of the most open pathways to entering the international job market. Unfortunately, few job seekers are familiar with this rather fascinating job market.

In this chapter we identify the major players in the international nonprofit job market. Late-comers to the World Wide Web, nonprofit organizations are finally using the Internet to publicize their causes, raise funds, and recruit volunteers and paid staff members. If you want to quickly get up and running with this international employment sector, you are well advised to explore the key gateway sites to the international nonprofit world as well as sample the websites of many nonprofit organizations we identify in this chapter. Numerous job opportunities with these organizations can be found posted on their websites. In addition, you should explore sites which specialize in job listings of nonprofit organizations.

For an extended discussion of the nonprofit employment world, including annotated descriptions of many employers, see our two companion volumes: ***Jobs and Careers With Nonprofit Organizations*** and the ***International Jobs Directory*** (impactpublications.com).

Gateway Nonprofit Websites

Several websites function as gateway sites to the nonprofit sector. Start with these sites for linkages to hundreds of nonprofits. The first two sites, idealist.org and guidestar.org, are incredibly comprehensive gateway sites to the nonprofit sector, both international and domestic.

Indeed, they may be the only two sites you need for connecting with the nonprofit sector.

- **Action Without Borders**   idealist.org
- **GuideStar**   guidestar.org
- **Internet Nonprofit Center**   nonprofits.org
- **Council on Foundations**   www.cof.org
- **Foundation Center**   fdncenter.org
- **Independent Sector**   indepsec.org
- **Impact Online**   impactonline.org
- **Charity Village**   charityvillage.com

The following websites function as online job boards for nonprofit employers and job seekers. They include hundreds of job vacancy announcements:

- **Access**   www.accessjobs.org
- **Community Career Center**   nonprofitjobs.org
- **Jobs For People Who Care**   www.jobsforpeoplewhocare.
                                   com

Guides to Nonprofit Employers

The following websites provide direct access to numerous international nonprofit organizations. Many of these websites include job announcements.

- **InterAction**   interaction.org
- **PACT**   pactworld.com
- **International Service**
  Agencies   charity.org
- **Intercrito**   jobleads.org
- **Global Health Council**   www.globalhealth.org
- **AIESEC**   aiesec.org
- **IAESTE**   iaeste.org
- **Volunteers for Peace**   www.vfp.org
- **JustAct (Youth Action**
  for Global Justice)   justact.org

InterAction.

American Council for Voluntary International Action

a COALITION of over 165 non-profit organizations working worldwide--and the U.S.'s **leading advocate** for sustainable development, refugee and disaster assistance and humanitarian aid.

Featured Member

ACTION HUNGER

INTERACTION MEMBERS

PRESS ROOM

NEWSWIRE

ABOUT INTERACTION

JOIN INTERACTION

INTERACTION MEMBERS RESPOND
How YOU Can Help!

InterAction Members Responding to:
Terrorist Attacks in US
Crisis in Afghanistan
Central America   Peru   HIV/AIDS
More...
Guide to Appropriate Giving
Save the Date! June 3-5
InterAction Forum 2002

InterAction Members

Sustainable Development

Disaster Response

Advocacy

| Home | Membership | Site Guide | Search |

GLOBAL HEALTH COUNCIL

because there is no them; only us

Join us to help save a million lives a year! | **Member Sign-In**

HEALTH NEWS

Monday, 31 December, 2001

News from Around the World

- **WHO Calls for Rise In Health Spending**
  A new report outlining the relationship between health and economic development calls for increased foreign aid spending by rich countries.

- **Ebola Kills Another in Central Africa**
  Another person has died of Ebola in Central Africa, bringing the death toll from an outbreak of the virus to 18.

About the Council
Who we are
Annual Conference
Annual Awards
Online Publications
Council News
Jobs at the Council

Membership
Join Us
Member Services
Members & Partners

 WORLD LEARNING

Now more than ever, peace through understanding.

International Development

Professional Training and Education

Language and Intercultural Training

Study Abroad and International Exchange

Graduate and Degree Programs

Extension and Certificate Programs

Peacebuilding and Social Justice

SIT Study Abroad students boost Belize villages devastated by hurricane

| Projects in International Development and Training | School for International Training | The Experiment in International Living | World Learning Business Solutions |

Major International Nonprofit Employers

The following nonprofit organizations have international operations in several countries around the world. They regularly hire individuals for both U.S.-based and field positions. Nonprofits followed with an asterisk (*) were recently (December 2001) selected by *Worth* magazine as among 100 best charities because of their ability to work with other groups, stay focused on their missions, and get things done through local leaders. Many of these organizations are very exciting international employers:

- Academy For Educational Development   aed.org
- ACCION International*   accion.org
- Adventist Development and Relief Agency International   adra.org
- Africare, Inc.   africare.org
- Agricultural Co-op Development International   www.acdivoca.org
- Air Serv International   www.airserv.org
- American Friends Service Committee   www.afsc.org
- American Jewish Joint Distribution Committee   ajc.org
- American Red Cross International Services   redcross.org/services/intl/
- American Refugee Committee*   archq.org
- AmeriCares Foundation   www.americares.org
- Amnesty International USA   amnesty-usa.org
- Ashoka*   ashoka.org
- Asia Foundation   asiafoundation.org
- Battelle Memorial Institute   www.battelle.org
- Bread for the World   bread.org
- Brother's Brother Foundation   brothersbrother.org
- CARE*   care.org
- Catholic Relief Services   catholicrelief.org

- Centre For Development
  and Population Activities   cedpa.org
- Childreach   www.childreach.org
- Christian Children's Fund   christianchildrensfund.org
- Church World Service   churchworldservice.org
- Compassion International   www.ci.org
- Conservation International*   conservation.org
- Direct Relief International*   directrelief.org
- Doctors Without Borders*   dwb.org
- Educational Development
  Center, Inc.   www.edc.org
- Esperanca, Inc.   esperanca.org
- Family Health International   www.fhi.org
- FINCA*   villagebanking.org
- Food For the Hungry, Inc.   fh.org
- Freedom From Hunger*   freedomfrom hunger.org
- Global Health Council   www.globalhealth.org
- Goodwill Industries
  International*   goodwill.org
- Greenpeace   greenpeaceusa.org
- Habitat for Humanity*   habitat.org
- Heifer International*   heifer.org
- Helen Keller International   www.hki.org
- The Hunger Project   www.thp.org
- Institute of International
  Education   www.iie.org
- InterExchange   interexchange.org
- International Aid   gospelcom.net/ia
- International Catholic
  Migration Commission   www.icmc.net
- International Center for
  Research on Women*   icrw.org
- International Development
  Enterprises   ideorg.org
- International Executive
  Service Corps   www.iesc.org
- International Eye Foundation   iefusa.org
- International Medical Corps*   imc-la.org

- International Rescue
  Committee   www.theirc.org
- LASPAU – Academic and
  Professional Programs for
  the Americas   www.laspau.harvard.edu
- Laubach Literacy
  International   laubach.org
- Lutheran Immigration
  and Refugee Service   www.lirs.org
- Lutheran World Relief   lwr.org
- MAP International   www.map.org
- Mennonite Central Committee   www.mcc.org
- Mercy Corps International*   mercycorps.org
- MidAmerica International
  Agricultural Consortium   miac.org
- National Wildlife Federation*   nwf.org
- The Nature Conservancy*   nature.org
- OIC (Opportunities Industrial
  Centers) International   oicinternational.org
- Operation USA*   opusa.org
- Opportunity International   www.opportunity.org
- Oxfam America*   oxfamamerica.org
- PACT (Private Agencies
  Collaborating Together)*   pactworld.org
- Partners of the Americas   www.partners.net
- Pathfinder International   www.pathfind.org
- People to People Health
  Foundation (Project HOPE)   projhope.org
- Physicians for Human Rights*   phrusa.org
- PLAN International   www.plan-international.org
- Planned Parenthood
  Federation   plannedparenthood.org
- Population Action
  International   populationaction.org
- Population Council   www.popcouncil.org
- Population Reference Bureau   www.prb.org
- Population Services
  International   www.psi.org

Bread for the World
Seeking Justice. Ending Hunger.

Bread for the World is a nationwide Christian citizens movement seeking justice for the world's hungry people by lobbying our nation's decision makers.

Find it here:

bulletin board
Congresslink
how to help
hunger basics
issues & action
jobs
Offering of Letters
online store
pressroom
site index
who we are

Legislative Action UPDATE

EXTRA EXTRA:
Africa: Hunger to Harvest passes Congress

Read all about it
Find out if your member supported the House bill and write a note of thanks

Hunger increased sharply, according to new report from U.S. Conference of Mayors

Bread for the World's 2002 Offering of Letters Campaign is gearing up for next year's kick-off.

Working from Poverty to Promise

About Our Website

Subscribe to our free eBread e-mail newsletter!
e-mail address
subscribe

Sign up to receive a free booklet.
What You Can Do to End Hunger

Order BFW Christmas cards through

Catholic Relief Services

...and the world...   In 2000, Catholic

daily reflection

What we believe

Where we work

Who we are

What we do

Emergencies

Contribute now

News Room

EMERGENCY RESPONSE

Afghan Regional Crisis
CRS is providing blankets and food to those in need.
Read more...

How to help   WHAT'S NEW

December 31, 2001

Search our site:
Go

Kids
Click Here

Home | contact us

childreach
Plan   BE A PART OF IT.

Helping children shape their world.
Be a part of it.

Welcome to Childreach, part of a unique global alliance of caring individuals like you – a worldwide community sharing a common agenda for child-centered development and the well-being, rights and interests of the world's children.

ABOUT CHILDREACH   WAYS TO HELP   SPONSOR A CHILD

A Day in the Life

- Program For Appropriate
  Technology in Health   path.org
- Project Concern
  International   projectconcern.org
- Research Triangle Institute   www.rti.org
- Refugees International*   refugeesinternational.org
- Salvation Army World
  Service Office   www.salvationarmy.org
- Save the Children
  Foundation, Inc.   savethechildren.org
- The Sierra Club   sierraclub.org
- Special Olympics*   specialolympics.org
- Technoserve*   tns.org
- U.S. Catholic Conference
  Office of Migration and
  Refugee Services   www.nccbuscc.org/mrs
- U.S. Fund for UNICEF*   unicefusa.org
- Unitarian Universalist
  Service Committee   www.uusc.org
- Volunteers in Overseas
  Cooperative Assistance   www.acdivoca.org
- Volunteers in Technical
  Assistance   www.acdivoca.org
- Winrock International
  Institute for Agricultural
  Development   www.winrock.org
- World Concern   worldconcern.org
- World Council of Credit
  Unions   www.woccu.org
- World Education   www.worlded.org
- World Relief Corporation   worldrelief.org
- World Resources Institute*   wri.org
- World Vision Relief and
  Development, Inc.   worldvision.org
- World Wildlife Fund*   worldwildlife.org
- Worldteach   worldteach.org
- Worldwatch Institute   worldwatch.org
- Y.M.C.A.   ymca.com

- Y.W.C.A.   www.ywca.org
- Zero Population Growth   zpg.org

Education, Research, and Associations

The following nonprofit education, research, and professional and trade organizations variously function as think tanks, lobbying groups, and training organizations. Most do a great deal of international work:

- American Enterprise Institute   www.aei.org
- Brookings Institution   brook.edu
- CATO Institute   cato.org
- Center for Strategic and
  International Studies (CSIS)   csis.org
- Chamber of Commerce   www.uschamber.org
- Council for International
  Exchange of Scholars   www.cies.org
- Council of the Americas   www.counciloftheamericas.
                                   org
- Council on Foreign Relations   cfr.org
- Council on International
  Educational Exchange (CIEE)   ciee.org
- Earthwatch Institute   earthwatch.org
- Foreign Policy Association   fpa.org
- Freedom House   freedomhouse.org
- Heritage Foundation   heritage.org
- Hoover Institute on War,
  Revolution, and Peace   hoover.org
- Hudson Institute   hudson.org
- Human Rights Watch   hrw.org
- The International Center   www.internationalcenter.
                                   com
- International Food Policy
  Research Institute   www.cgiar.org
- International Schools Services   iss.edu
- Meridian International Center   www.meridian.org
- NAFSA/Association of
  International Educators   nafsa.org

- Near East Foundation   neareast.org
- Overseas Development
  Council   odc.org
- RAND Corporation   www.rand.org
- Rodale Institute   rodaleinstitute.org
- U.S.-China Business Council www.uschina.org
- United States Olympic
  Committee   olympic-usa.org
- The Urban Institute   www.urban.org
- World Learning   www.worldlearning.org
- World Neighbors   wn.org
- Youth For Understanding
  International Exchange   www.yfu.org

9

Government Opportunities

THE UNITED STATES FEDERAL GOVERNMENT OFFERS numerous international job opportunities for individuals who understand various agencies as well as the whole hiring process. Dozens of agencies, from the U.S. State Department to the U.S. Postal Service, have international missions as well as a presence abroad. They regularly hire for both entry-level and senior-level international positions.

The key to landing an international job with a federal agency is to understand how it operates. Since a great deal of agency information, including job vacancy announcements, is now available online, you can quickly survey international operations and opportunities in the federal government by visiting various websites that focus on the work of agencies and the application process.

Gateway Websites

If you are unfamiliar with the workings of the federal government, you are well advised to visit several gateway sites that explore both agencies and job opportunities throughout the federal government. A few key sites will take you on a quick tour of the federal government as well as provide you with instant access to hundreds of job vacancies available each day. Some of these sites also will help you prepare a well-focused federal resume or OF-612 to apply for such jobs. Gateway websites for accessing information on federal agencies, as well as job listings, include the following:

- **The White House**   whitehouse.gov
- **FedGate**   fedgate.org
- **FedWorld**   www.fedworld.gov
- **USA Jobs**   usajobs.opm.gov
- **Federal Jobs Central**   fedjobs.com
- **Federal Jobs Digest**   jobsfed.com

Other websites include federal, state, and local government jobs in the United States as well as government jobs in other countries. Several of these sites also deal with law enforcement jobs:

- **911hotjobs.com**   lawenforcementjobs.com
- **Careers in Government**   careersingovernment.com
- **Careers in Law Enforcement**   lejobs.com
- **Classified Employment
  Web Site**   www.yourinfosource.com
- **Cop Career.com**   copcareer.com
- **Corrections.com**   database.corrections.com/
                                       career
- **Federal Jobs Net**   federaljobs.net
- **Federal Job Search**   federaljobsearch.com
- **Federal Times**   federaltimes.com
- **FirstGov**   firstgov.gov
- **GovernmentJobs.com**   governmentjobs.com
- **Govjobs.com**   govjobs.com
- **Govtjob.net**   govtjob.net
- **Jobs4PublicSector (Europe)**   jobs4publicsector.com
- **LawEnforcementJob.com**   lawenforcementjob.com
- **Officer.Com**   officer.com
- **PoliceCareer.com**   policecareer.com
- **PSE-NET.com**   PSE-NET.com

- StateJobs.com   statejobs.com
- United Nations   www.unsystem.org
- US Government Jobs.com usgovernmentjobs.com

Application Process and Resources

There's a lot more to applying for a federal job than just accessing information online. For more detailed information on federal jobs, including tips on completing a federal resume, an OF-612, and other forms, be sure to check out these publications:

> *The Book of U.S. Government Jobs* (Dennis V. Damp)
> *The Directory of Federal Jobs and Employers* (Ron and Caryl Krannich)
> *Federal Applications That Get Resumes* (Russ Smith)
> *Federal Resume Guidebook* (Kathy Troutman)
> *Find a Federal Job Fast!* (Ron and Caryl Krannich)
> *International Jobs Directory* (Ron and Caryl Krannich)

They will give you an inside look at the whole hiring process as well as the type of language that is required when communicating your qualifications to federal agencies. Most of them are available through Impact Publications (impactpublications.com).

You also can download various federal application forms by going directly to the electronic forms section of the U. S. Office of Personnel Management's website:

opm.gov/forms

Consider the "Big Five" and Others

The federal government offers thousands of international job opportunities. The largest number of international jobs are found with the "big five" federal agencies that have major international missions:

- U.S. Department of State   state.gov
- U.S. Department of Defense   www.defenselink.mil

- U.S. Agency for International
  Development (USAID)   www.usaid.gov
- Peace Corps   peacecorps.com
- Central Intelligence Agency   www.cia.gov

Other federal government departments and agencies with international positions include the following:

- African Development
  Foundation   www.adf.gov
- Consumer Product Safety
  Commission   cpsc.gov
- Department of Agriculture   www.usda.gov
- Department of Commerce   www.doc.gov
- Department of Energy   energy.gov
- Department of Health
  and Human Services   www.os.dhhs.gov
- Department of Justice   www.usdoj.gov
- Department of
  Transportation   www.dot.gov
- Environmental Protection
  Agency   epa.gov
- Export-Import Bank   exim.gov
- Federal Communications
  Commission   www.fcc.gov
- Federal Emergency
  Management Agency   www.fema.gov
- General Services
  Administration   gsa.gov
- Immigration and
  Naturalization Service   www.ins.usdoj.gov
- Inter-American Foundation   www.iaf.gov
- Internal Revenue Service   www.irs.ustreas.gov
- Smithsonian Institution   www.si.edu
- U.S. Postal Service   www.usps.gov

Check the Invaluable USAID Network

When looking to the government for international employment opportunities, be sure to do your homework. Learn as much as possible about the agencies by visiting their websites and by networking with individuals who are familiar with the agency. Keep in mind that government agencies contract out a deal of work. Try to discover whom they work with on international matters.

Unfortunately, many federal government agencies experience temporary hiring freezes that both delay and disappoint job seekers. USAID, for example, has undergone a great deal of downsizing and experiences frequent hiring freezes. Indeed, this agency is a shadow of what it used to be a decade or two ago. Much of its work is contracted out. Therefore, you may want to contact many of the firms that do work with USAID (see Chapter 10). Many contractors offer excellent international job opportunities. You can identify these firms through USAID's website (www.usaid.gov), which lists its contractors in the *USAID Yellow Book*. USAID also maintains a useful list of "Development Links" on its website:

www.usaid.gov/about/resources

This section will take you directly to many of the major federal government agencies, non-governmental and private voluntary organizations, international and regional organizations, and foreign government agencies that work with USAID.

International and Regional Organizations

The United Nations and other international organizations also provide a wealth of international job and career opportunities. For U.S. citizens, a good starting point is the U.S. Department of State, which maintains a listing of international job vacancies through its Bureau of International Organizations. It includes a biweekly listing of "International Vacancy Announcements – United Nations and Other International Organizations":

state.gov/p/io/empl

World Health Organization

Home · Health topics A to Z · WHO as an Organization · Site Index · Search

Director-General's Office

Biography of the Director-General and text of all the Director-General's speeches.

More info

Information resources

Library. Publications Catalogue. Multimedia resources. Individual publications such as the Bulletin, Weekly Epidemiological Record, World Health Report, ICD-10 Classification scheme.

More info

Press Media Centre

CURRENT WHO INFORMATION ON:

Ebola outbreak in Gabon and Congo

The Central Asia Crisis

Biological and Chemical Weapons

Investment in global health will generate substantial returns says Commission on Macroeconomics and Health

20 December 2001 | London -- After two years of work, the Commission on Macroeconomics and Health today presented its report on investing in health for economic development to WHO. This group of leading economists and health

Upcoming Events

Tobacco-free 2002 Winter Olympics

8-24 February 2002 / Salt Lake City, Utah (USA)

TOBACCO FREE SPORTS

The XIX Olympic Winter Games and the VIII Paralympic Winter Games in Salt Lake City will be tobacco free events. In a bold move which will protect smokers and non-smokers alike, the use and sale of tobacco products will be prohibited.

Tobacco Free Initiative

IBRD · IDA · IFC · MIGA · ICSID

Contact Us · Help/FAQ · Index · Search

The World Bank Group
Our Dream is a World Free of Poverty

Search [   ] GO

More Options

Main Sections

About Us

Countries & Regions

Data & Statistics

Development Topics

Documents & Reports

Evaluation - OED

Learning - WB Institute

What's New

Friday, December 28, 2001

Building Infrastructure, Tackling Poverty

A sample of Bank's work in Latin America

▶ Papua New Guinea: World Bank Approves The Release Of The Second Tranche Under The Governance Promotion Adjustment Loan - Dec. 21, 2001

▶ DR Congo Donor Technical Update Meeting - Dec.

Poverty In Focus

Globalization, Growth and Poverty

Globalization Must Work for the Poor

...more

Events

Development Marketplace - Jan. 9 - 10, 2002

United Nations Environment Programme

UNEP   Programme des Nations Unies pour l'environnement

Site Locator | Support UNEP | Contacts |

Nairobi, Tuesday, January 01, 2002

Search UNEP [go!]

The Organization
About UNEP
Executive Director
Conventions/Treaties
Publications
Events and Awards
Children & Youth
Jobs/Training
Annual Report
Support UNEP
Photo Gallery

International effort to pin point some of the world's best solar and wind power sites gets underway

Findings should boost prospects for renewable energy across the globe

Nairobi/Paris, 18 December 2001 · A pioneering project to map the solar and wind resource of 13 developing countries is launched today by the United Nations Environment Programme. Experts are convinced that the project, called the Solar and Wind Energy Survey Assessment (SWERA), will prove that the potential for deploying solar panels and wind turbines in these countries is far greater than is currently supposed

Full Story...

Organogram

Executive Director

UNEP Divisions ▾

Media Room
Welcome
Press Releases
Information Notes
Speeches

Products & Services

EarthPrint

You also may want to contact various international agencies directly. The following site functions as a directory to the United Nations system. Its sub-site also includes information on careers with the United Nations, including vacancy announcements:

- **United Nations System**   www.unsystem.org
- **Vacancy Announcements**   icsc.un.org/vab/index.htm

Within the United Nations, the following agencies are especially popular for job seekers:

- **U.N. Secretariat**   www.un.org/Depts/OHRM
- **U.N. Development
  Program (UNDP)**   www.undp.org
- **U.N. Development Fund
  for Women**   www.unifem.undp.org
- **United Nations Volunteers**   www.unv.org
- **U.N. High Commissioner
  for Refugees (UNHCR)**   www.unhcr.ch
- **U.N. Environment
  Programme (UNEP)**   www.unep.org
- **U.N. Institute for Training
  and Research (UNITAR)**   www.unitar.org
- **U.N. Fund for Population
  Activities**   www.unfpa.org
- **U.N. Educational, Scientific,
  and Cultural Organization
  (UNESCO)**   www.unesco.org
- **Food and Agriculture
  Organization (FAO)**   www.fao.org
- **The World Bank**   worldbank.org
- **International Monetary
  Fund (IMF)**   www.imf.org
- **International Finance
  Corporation (IFC)**   www.ifc.org
- **International Fund for
  Agricultural Development
  (IFAD)**   www.ifad.org

- International Labour
  Organization (ILO)   ilo.org
- World Health
  Organization (WHO)   who.int

Several other major international organizations, which are primarily financial or security institutions, are worth exploring for interesting job opportunities:

- African Development Bank   afdb.org
- Asian Development Bank   adb.org
- Inter-American
  Development Bank   www.iadb.org
- European Investment Bank   www.eib.org
- Organization of American
  States (OAS)   oas.org
- North Atlantic Treaty
  Organisation (NATO)   www.nato.int
- Organisation for Economic
  Co-operation and
  Development   www.oecd.org
- Consultative Group on
  International Agricultural
  Research   cgiar.org
- Pan American Health
  Organization   www.paho.org
- Pacific Community   www.spc.org.nc
- Inter-American Institute for
  Cooperation on Agriculture   iicanet.org
- International
  Organization for Migration   www.iom.int
- International Atomic
  Energy Agency   www.iaea.or.at

10

Contracting and Consulting Firms

MANY CONSULTING AND CONTRACTING FIRMS, which are primarily based in the U.S., work with a wide variety of international-oriented organizations. Some of these firms are mainly oriented toward the development work of USAID, the World Bank, the United Nations, and regional governmental groups. Other firms are more business oriented.

Government Contractors

Many of the following firms assist major international funding agencies, such as USAID, the World Bank, IMF, and the United Nations. Firms, such as Louis Berger International, Development Alternatives Inc., Checchi and Company Consulting, Robert R. Nathan Associates, and Creative Associates International are noted for their innovative development work in Third World countries:

- **ABB Lummus Global**   abb.com/lummus
- **Abt Associates, Inc.**   www.abtassoc.com

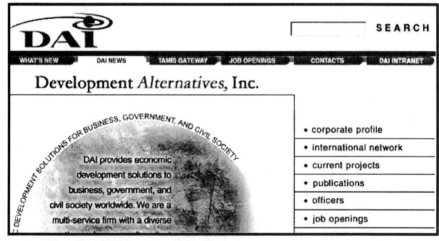

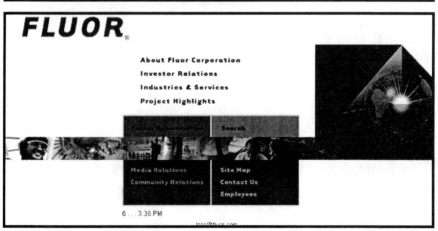

- Advanced Systems
  Development   asd-inc.com
- American Institutes for
  Research   www.air-dc.org
- AMEX International, Inc.   amexdc.com
- ARD, Inc.   www.ardinc.com
- Arkel International, Ltd.   arkel.com
- Automation Research
  Systems, Ltd.   arslimited.com
- Bechtel Group, Inc.   www.bechtel.com
- R.W. Beck, Inc.   www.rwbeck.com
- Louis Berger Group, Inc.   louisberger.com
- Birch & Davis   www.birchdavis.com
- Black and Veatch   www.bv.com/bv
- Booz Allen Hamilton   bah.com
- John T. Boyd Company   www.jtboyd.com
- Boyle Engineering Corp.   boyleengineering.com
- Buchart-Horn, Inc.   bh-ba.com
- Burns and Roe Enterprises   www.roe.com
- CACI International. Inc.   www.caci.com
- Camp Dresser & McKee,
  Inc.   www.cdm.com
- Carter & Burgess, Inc.   www.ftp.c-b.com
- CBI Industries, Inc.   www.chicagobridge.com
- Checchi and Company
  Consulting, Inc.   www.checchiconsulting.com
- Chemonics International   chemonics.com
- Conservation International   conservation.org
- Creative Associates
  International, Inc.   caii-dc.com
- Development Alternatives,
  Inc.   www.dai.com
- Development Associates, Inc.   www.devassoc1.com
- Dillingham Construction
  Corp.   www.dillingham construction.com
- DMJM + Harris, Inc.   www.dmjmharris.com
- DPRA, Inc.   www.dpra.com
- Earth Satellite Corporation   www.earthsat.com

- Engineering-Science, Inc.   parsons.com
- Fluor Corporation   fluor.com
- Foster Wheeler
  International Corp.   www.fwc.com
- The Futures Group
  International   www.tfgi.com
- Gannett Fleming   gannettfleming.com
- Heery International, Inc.   heery.com
- Hellmuth, Obata&
  Kassabaum   hok.com
- International Resources
  Group, Ltd.   irgltd.com
- John Snow, Inc.   www.jsi.com
- Labat-Anderson, Inc.   www.labat.com
- LTS Corporation.   ltscorporation.com
- Mathtech, Inc.   mathtechinc.com
- Metcalf & Eddy
  International   www.m-e.com
- MMM Design Group   www.mmmdesigngroup.com
- Montgomery Watson Harza   www.mwhglobal.com
- Morrison-Maierle/CSSA, Inc.   m-m.net
- Multi Consult Milano   www.multiconsult.com
- Nathan Associates   nathanassoc.com
- Navigant Consulting, Inc.   www.rmiinc.com
- PADCO, Inc.   www.padcoinc.com
- Parsons Corporation   parsons.com
- Parsons Brinckerhoff
  International   www.pbworld.com
- Pragma Corporation   pragmacorp.com
- Raytheon Engineering &
  Construction   www.raytheon.com
- Sheladia Associates, Inc.   sheladia.com
- Washington Group
  International   www.wgint.com
- Wilbur Smith Associates,
  Inc.   wilbursmith.com
- SRI International   sri.com
- STV Group   wstvinc.com

- TAMS Consultants, Inc.   www.tamsconsultants.com
- University Research
  Corporation   www.urc-chs.com
- Washington Consulting
  Group   www.washcg.com
- Wimberly Allison Tong
  & Goo   watg.com

Business Consulting Firms

The major international consulting firms, which primarily work in the private sector but also do some government and nonprofit work, include the following companies. Many of these highly competitive firms, such as the Boston Consulting Group, are known for their cutting-edge international work and are famous for being some of the best companies to work for in terms of salaries, benefits, advancement opportunities, and corporate cultures. BCG's website (bcg.com) offers useful information on the company as well as the job search in general:

- Boston Consulting Group   bcg.com
- Andersen   andersen.com
- Arthur D. Little Inc.   www.adlittle.com
- Bain and Company   bain.com
- Booz Allen Hamilton   bah.com
- Deloitte and Touche   dttus.com
- Ernst & Young   ey.com
- Hay Group, Inc.   haygroup.com
- Hewitt Associates   www.hewitt.com
- Hill & Knowlton   www.hillandknowlton.com
- KPMG   kpmg.com
- McKinsey and Co. Inc.   mckinsey.com
- PricewaterhouseCoopers   pwcglobal.com

Teaching Jobs Overseas
International Employment for Teachers

Joy Jobs .com

 Teaching Jobs Overseas Topics: international teaching, teaching overseas, teaching abroad, American and international schools, overseas jobs, international employment, etc.

Community   Jobs   Recruitment   Reference

Jobs. Schools. Employment Information:

▸ **Where the real jobs are**
The all-you-ever-need overseas info package

▸ **International Community**
Teaching overseas: pros and cons. Options and opinions

- **Talk Back** *"your site is idiotic"*
  "I went to the UNI conference and thought it was horrible"

▸ **Getting your foot in the door**
Here's how

▸ **How it works**

LOGIN

European Council of International Schools

Home   Login   Links   Search / Find   Events   Contact Us

Wednesday, 2 January 2002

happy holidays

Welcome to the ECIS website

Our search engine will quickly and easily find whatever you are looking for on this site. Navigate the site using the top bar and the links on the left of each page.

Professional Development

Recruitment Services

Membership

Information Service

Starting a New School

About ECIS

IStA Homepage

ECIS

Early Childhood Conference, Building Our Future: One Child at a Time at the American School of Dubai, 24-25 January 2002. Click here for more information. **Registration** extended!

ECIS Restructuring Project ... and the establishment of CIS in 2002/3. Newly updated information, October 2001. Click here to read it now.

Services
for Schools
for Educators
for Colleges
for Parents
for Students

Find
a Job
a School
a University
Supplies/
Services

In-Service
Conferences

International Schools Services

Welcome

Providing services to overseas schools and meeting the educational needs of companies abroad has been the business of International Schools Services for over 40 years.

ISS plans, designs, and manages schools, and offers extensive consulting services for companies with operations around the world. In addition we provide teacher and

Who

Services

School Management

Recruitment Services

Resources

Publications

Contact

The Source

11

Teaching Abroad

E ACH YEAR THOUSANDS OF INTERNATIONAL JOB seekers move abroad to teach. From elementary to higher education, as English and science teachers to school administrators, they find the field of education to be one of the easiest and most rewarding ways to acquire international experience. For many individuals, teaching is a good entry point for launching either a short- or long-term international career. As a result, numerous websites specialize in helping individuals find jobs in education, with special emphasis on teaching English abroad.

Elementary to Secondary Education

The following organizations focus on international education, with primary emphasis on elementary, middle, and high schools, both public and private. Organizations such as the International Schools Services (iss.edu) operate a network of over 500 international schools around the globe. The U.S. State Department and the U.S. Department of Defense, which operate their own schools in dozens of countries, hire U.S. citizens to provide educational services in these schools. Taken together, these U.S.-based organizations offer some of the most attractive American-style teaching and administrative positions in elementary to secondary education. They recruit for all teaching subjects and administrative talents. Other organizations, such as the University of Iowa and Search Associates, offer placement services. If you're looking for a good gateway site for teaching abroad, be sure to focus on our first selection, joyjobs.com.

- **Teaching Jobs Overseas**   joyjobs.com
- **International Schools Services**   iss.edu
- **WWTeach.com**   wwteach.com
- **European Council of International Schools**   ecis.org
- **Ed-U-Link Services, Inc.**   edulink.com
- **Search Associates**   search-associates.com
- **Friends of World Teaching**   fowt.com
- **Institute of International Education**   www.iie.org
- **University of Iowa Overseas Placement Service**   www.uni.edu/placemnt/overseas
- **Association of American Schools in South America (AASSA)**   aassa.com
- **Education Jobs in the UK**   www.education-jobs.co.uk
- **Transitions Abroad**   transitionsabroad.com
- **NAFSA: Association of International Educators**   nafsa.org
- **U.S. State Department (Office of Overseas Schools)**   state.gov/m/a/os
- **U.S. Department of Defense Educational Activity**   www.odedodea.edu

Higher Education

If your international education interests lie in higher education, you should check out several of the following sites. If you are a U.S. citizen and currently teach at a U.S. university or are a graduate student at a participating institution, you may want to apply for a Fulbright teaching position. Contact your university as well as the Council for International Exchange of Scholars (www.iie.org/cies) for eligibility requirements and application information.

- **Chronicle of Higher Education** — thisweek.chronicle.com
- **University of Maryland (Overseas teaching program)** — umuc.edu/internat/facinfo. html
- **Association of Commonwealth Universities** — www.acu.ac.uk
- **Times Higher Education Supplement** — www.thesis.co.uk
- **United Nations University** — www.unu.edu

Teaching English

Teaching English remains one of the easiest ways to land an international job. English teaching jobs are plentiful in Asia, especially in Japan, Korea, Taiwan, Hong Kong, China, and Thailand. The following sites primarily focus on teaching English abroad:

- **Dave's ESL Café** — eslcafe.com
- **ELT Job Center** — www.edunet.com/jobs/index. html
- **SISA America** — ybmsisa.com
- **TESOL** — tesol.org
- **JET Program** — www.clair.nippon-net.ne.jp/ html_e/jet/general.htm
- **Internet/Networks (Mexico)** — employnow.com/Mexico.htm
- **TEFL/TESL Jobs Worldwide** — tefl.net/jobs
- **ESLworldwide.com** — eslworldwide.com
- **Educational Services International (China)** — www.esiadventure.org
- **ELIC (China)** — www.elic.org
- **AEON (Japan)** — aeonet.com
- **O-Hayo Sensei (Japan)** — ohayosensei.com
- **ESL Korea** — eslkorea.com
- **Teach in Thailand** — teach-in-thailand.com

- Teach in Taiwan   teach-in-taiwan.com
- Goal Asia   goalasia.com

Index

The Authors

OR NEARLY TWO DECADES DRS. RON AND CARYL Krannich have pursued a passion – assisting hundreds of thousands of individuals, from students, the unemployed, and ex-offenders to military personnel, international job seekers, and CEOs, in making critical job and career transitions. Focusing on key job search skills, career changes, and employment fields, their impressive body of work has helped shape career thinking and behavior both in the United States and abroad. Their sound advice has changed numerous lives, including their own!

Ron and Caryl are two of America's leading career and travel writers who have authored more than 60 books. A former Peace Corps Volunteer and Fulbright Scholar, Ron received his Ph.D. in Political Science from Northern Illinois University. Caryl received her Ph.D. in Speech Communication from Penn State University. Together they operate Development Concepts Incorporated, a training, consulting, and publishing firm in Virginia.

The Krannichs are both former university professors, high school teachers, management trainers, and consultants. As trainers and consultants, they have completed numerous projects on management, career development, local government, population planning, and rural development in the United States and abroad. Their career books focus on key job search skills, military and civilian career transitions, government and international careers, travel jobs, and nonprofit organizations. Their books represent one of today's most comprehensive collections of career writing. With over 2 million copies in print, their publications are widely available in bookstores, libraries, and career centers. No strangers to the Internet world, Ron and Caryl have been instrumental in publishing several Internet recruitment and job search books as well as developing career-related websites: impactpublications.com, winningthejob.com, contentforcareers.com, veteransworld.com, and greentogray.com. Many of their career tips appear on such major websites as monster.com, careerbuilder.com, careerweb.com, and campuscareercenter.com.

Ron and Caryl live a double life with travel being their best kept *"do what you love"* career secret. Authors of 19 travel-shopping guidebooks on various destinations around the world, they continue to pursue their international and travel interests through their innovative **Treasures and Pleasures of . . . Best of the Best** travel-shopping series and related websites: ishoparoundtheworld.com and contentfortravel.com. When not found at their home and business in Virginia, they are probably somewhere in Europe, Asia, Africa, the Middle East, the South Pacific, or the Caribbean and South America pursuing their other passion – researching and writing about quality arts and antiques as well as following the advice of their other Click and Easy™ volume designed for road warriors and other travel types: **Travel Planning on the Internet: The Click and Easy™ Guide**. *"We follow the same career and life-changing advice we give to others – pursue a passion that enables you to do what you really love to do,"* say the Krannichs.

As both career and travel experts, the Krannichs' work is frequently featured in major newspapers, magazines, and newsletters as well as on radio, television, and the Internet. Available for interviews, consultation, and presentations, they can be contacted as follows:

Ron and Caryl Krannich
krannich@impactpublications.com

Career Resources

THE FOLLOWING CAREER RESOURCES ARE AVAILABLE directly from Impact Publications. Complete the following form or list the titles, include postage (see formula at the end), enclose payment, and send your order to:

IMPACT PUBLICATIONS
9104 Manassas Drive, Suite N
Manassas Park, VA 20111-5211
1-800-361-1055 (orders only)
Tel. 703-361-7300 or Fax 703-335-9486
Email address: *orders@impactpublications.com*
Quick & easy online ordering: www.impactpublications.com

Orders from individuals must be prepaid by check, moneyorder, or credit card. We accept telephone, fax, and email orders.

Qty.	TITLES	Price	TOTAL

Internet

Qty.	TITLES	Price	TOTAL
____	100 Top Internet Job Sites	$12.95	____
____	America's Top Internet Job Sites	19.95	____
____	CareerXroads (annual)	26.95	____
____	**Directory of Websites for International Jobs**	19.95	____
____	Guide to Internet Job Searching	14.95	____
____	Haldane's Best Employment Websites for Professionals	15.95	____
____	Job Search Online For Dummies	24.99	____
____	Travel Planning on the Internet	19.95	____

Career Exploration and Assessment

Qty.	TITLES	Price	TOTAL
____	Change Your Job, Change Your Life	17.95	____
____	Discover the Best Jobs For You	15.95	____
____	What Color Is Your Parachute?	16.95	____

Networking

Qty.	TITLES	Price	TOTAL
____	A Foot in the Door	14.95	____
____	Masters of Networking	16.95	____
____	The Savvy Networker	14.95	____

Resumes and Letters

___	Best Resumes and CVs for International Jobs	24.95	___
___	Haldane's Best Cover Letters For Professionals	15.95	___
___	Haldane's Best Resumes For Professionals	15.95	___
___	High Impact Resumes & Letters	19.95	___
___	Resumes For Dummies	14.99	___

Interviews and Salary Negotiations

___	101 Dynamite Answers to Interview Questions	12.95	___
___	101 Dynamite Questions to Ask At Your Job Interview	13.95	___
___	Dynamite Salary Negotiations	15.95	___
___	Haldane's Best Answers to Tough Interview Questions	15.95	___
___	Haldane's Best Salary Tips for Professionals	15.95	___
___	Interview For Success	15.95	___

International and Travel Jobs

___	Global Resume and CV Guide	17.95	___
___	Inside Secrets to Finding a Career in Travel	14.95	___
___	International Jobs Directory	19.95	___
___	Work Abroad	15.95	___

SUBTOTAL ___

Virginia residents add 4½% sales tax ___

POSTAGE/HANDLING ($5 for first
product and 8% of SUBTOTAL) $5.00

8% of SUBTOTAL --- ___

TOTAL ENCLOSED ---------------------------- ___

SHIP TO:

NAME _____

ADDRESS _____

_____

_____

PAYMENT METHOD:

❑ I enclose check/moneyorder for $ _____ made payable to
IMPACT PUBLICATIONS.

❑ Please charge $ _____ to my credit card:
❑ Visa ❑ MasterCard ❑ American Express ❑ Discover

Card # _____

Expiration date: _____/_____

Signature _____

Connect To the Net

for all your career and travel resource needs!